U.S. Department
of Transportation

**Federal Aviation
Administration**

FAA-S-8081-12C
(with changes 1, 2, 3, & 4)

Commercial Pilot
Practical Test Standards
for
Airplane
(SEL, MEL, SES, MES)

November 2011
(Effective June 1, 2012)

Flight Standards Service
Washington, DC 20591

(this page intentionally left blank)

Commercial Pilot
Airplane
Practical Test Standards

2011

Flight Standards Service
Washington, DC 20591

Note

Material in FAA-S-8081-12C will be **effective June 1, 2012**. All previous editions of the Commercial Pilot—Airplane Practical Test Standards will be obsolete as of this date.

Foreword

The Commercial Pilot—Airplane Practical Test Standards (PTS) book has been published by the Federal Aviation Administration (FAA) to establish the standards for commercial pilot certification practical tests for the airplane category, single-engine land and sea; and multiengine land and sea classes. FAA inspectors and designated pilot examiners shall conduct practical tests in compliance with these standards. Flight instructors and applicants should find these standards helpful during training and when preparing for the practical test.

/s/ Raymond Towles 11/3/2011

_____

for John Allen, Director
Flight Standards Service

(this page intentionally left blank)

Record of Changes

Change 1 (March 13, 2012)

- Removed Judgment Assessment Matrix.
  - **Reason:** Did not apply to this PTS

Change 2 (March 23, 2012)

- Added criterion number 9 to Section 1, Area of Operation IV, Task A Objective.
  - **Reason:** Inadvertently omitted during last revision.

- Added criterion number 9 to Section 2, Area of Operation IV, Task A Objective.
  - **Reason:** Inadvertently omitted during last revision.

Change 3 (May 1, 2012)

- Added Task F to the additional ratings held for Area of Operation II in the Airplane Multiengine Land column of the Additional Ratings Task Table: Airplane Single-Engine Land.
  - **Reason:** Recommendation from inspector in the field.

- Added Task C to the additional ratings held for Area of Operation IX in the Airplane Single-Engine Sea column of the Additional Ratings Task Table: Airplane Single-Engine Land.
  - **Reason:** Recommendation from inspector in the field.

- Added Task C to the additional ratings held for Area of Operation IX in the Airplane Multiengine Land column of the Additional Ratings Task Table: Airplane Single-Engine Land.
  - **Reason:** Recommendation from inspector in the field.

- Added Task C to the additional ratings held for Area of Operation IX in the Airplane Multiengine Sea column of the Additional Ratings Task Table: Airplane Single-Engine Land.
  - **Reason:** Recommendation from inspector in the field.

- Added Task C to the additional ratings held for Area of Operation IX in the Airplane Single-Engine Land column of the Additional Ratings Task Table: Airplane Single-Engine Sea.
  - **Reason:** Recommendation from inspector in the field.

- Added Task C to the additional ratings held for Area of Operation IX in the Airplane Multiengine Land column of the Additional Ratings Task Table: Airplane Single-Engine Sea.
  - **Reason:** Recommendation from inspector in the field.

- Added Task C to the additional ratings held for Area of Operation IX in the Airplane Multiengine Sea column of the Additional Ratings Task Table: Airplane Single-Engine Sea.
  - **Reason:** Recommendation from inspector in the field.

- Revised Note in Section 1, Area of Operation VIII.
  - **Reason:** Recommendation from inspector in the field.

- Revised criterion number 6 in Section 1, Area of Operation VIII, Task B Objective.
  - **Reason:** Recommendation from inspector in the field.

- Revised criterion number 6 in Section 1, Area of Operation VIII, Task C Objective.
  - **Reason:** Recommendation from inspector in the field.

- Revised criterion number 6 in Section 1, Area of Operation VIII, Task D Objective.
  - **Reason:** Recommendation from inspector in the field.

- Revised Note in Section 2, Area of Operation VII.
  - **Reason:** Recommendation from inspector in the field.

- Revised criterion number 6 in Section 2, Area of Operation VII, Task B Objective.
  - **Reason:** Recommendation from inspector in the field.

- Revised criterion number 6 in Section 2, Area of Operation VII, Task C Objective.
  - **Reason:** Recommendation from inspector in the field.

- Revised criterion number 6 in Section 2, Area of Operation VII, Task D Objective.
  - o **Reason:** Recommendation from inspector in the field.

Change 4 (September 20, 2012)

- Corrected 14 CFR part number in Element 8 of "Commercial Pilot – Airplane Practical Test Prerequisites" section of Introduction
  - o **Reason:** Part number previously stated was incorrect.

Commercial Pilot Practical Test Standards for Airplane (FAA-S-8081-12C) (with changes 1, 2, 3, & 4) Note

An errata sheet indicating the content and grammatical errors discovered in this document since its publication is located at the following web address:

http://www.faa.gov/training_testing/testing/test_standards/

These errors will be corrected in the next version of the document.

Errata as of November 7, 2012

1. In the last sentence of the Positive Exchange of Flight Controls section of the Introduction (page 18), "by" should be changed to "be."

Errata as of November 29, 2012

1. In the last sentence of the Flight Instructor Responsibility section of the Introduction (page 11), "manufacture's" should be changed to "manufacturer's."
2. In Section 1, Area of Operation IV, Task E, Objective 7 (page 46), "proposing" should be changed to "porpoising."
3. In Section 1, Area of Operation IV, Task I, Objective 5 (page 49), "proposing" should be changed to "porpoising."
4. In Section 2, Area of Operation I, Task I, Objective 3 (page 91), "proposing" should be changed to "porpoising."
5. In Section 2, Area of Operation II, Task E, Objective 6 (page 94), "proposing" should be changed to "porpoising."
6. In Section 2, Area of Operation IV, Task A, Objective 8 (page 99), "proposing" should be changed to "porpoising."
7. In Section 2, Area of Operation IV, Task C, Objective 7 (page 101), "proposing" should be changed to "porpoising."
8. In Section 2, Area of Operation IV, Task E, Objective 5 (page 103), "proposing" should be changed to "porpoising."
9. In Section 2, Area of Operation IV, Task G, Objective 5 (page 104), "proposing" should be changed to "porpoising."

Errata as of December 21, 2012

1. In the Major Enhancements to Version FAA-S-8081-12C for Section 1, "Task K, Forward Slip to a Landing" should be removed.
2. In the Major Enhancements to Version FAA-S-8081-12C for Section 1, "Task L" should be changed to "Task K".
3. In the Major Enhancements to Version FAA-S-8081-12C for Section 1, "Task M" should be changed to "Task L".

Errata as of January 7, 2013

1. In the first sentence of the 3rd paragraph in the Examiner Responsibility section of the Introduction (page 12), "lift off" should be changed to "liftoff."
2. In the last sentence of the 3rd paragraph in the Examiner Responsibility section of the Introduction (page 12), "500 feet AGL" should be changed to "400 feet AGL."
3. In the Note for Section 2, Area of Operation VIII, Task C (page 114), "VSSE/VXSE/VYSE" should be changed to "$V_{SSE}/V_{XSE}/V_{YSE}$."
4. In the Note for Section 2, Area of Operation VIII, Task C (page 114), "500 feet AGL" should be changed to "400 feet AGL."

Errata as of July 10, 2013

1. In the references listed in the Practical Test Standards Description section of the Introduction (page 3), "AC 91-69 Cold Weather Operation of Aircraft" should be changed to "AC 91-13 Cold Weather Operation of Aircraft."

Errata as of January 8, 2014

1. In the *Removal of the "Limited to Center Thrust" Limitation* section of the Introduction (page 8), "Area of Operation IX: Emergency Operations" should be changed to "Area of Operation VIII: Emergency Operations" and "Area of Operation XI: Multiengine Operations" should be changed to "Area of Operation X: Multiengine Operations."

Major Enhancements to Version FAA-S-8081-12C

- All references reviewed and updated throughout.
- Introduction:

  o Abbreviations Sections added
  o Use of Practical Test Standards updated
  o Use of the Judgment Assessment Matrix added
  o Special Emphasis Areas updated
  o Removal of the "Limited to Center Thrust" Limitations added
  o Commercial Pilot—Airplane Practical Test Prerequisites updated
  o Use of FAA-Approved Flight Simulator or Flight Training Device
  o Flight Instructor Responsibility updated
  o Examiner Responsibility updated
  o Satisfactory Performance updated
  o Single-Pilot Resource Management updated
  o Aeronautical Decision-Making added
  o Risk Management added
  o Task Management added
  o Situational Awareness added
  o Controlled Flight Into Terrain Awareness added
  o Automation Management added
  o Letter of Discontinuance added
  o Applicant's Use of Checklists updated
  o Stalls and Spin Awareness added

Section 1, Commercial Pilot—Airplane (Single-Engine Land and Single-Engine Sea)

- Additional Rating Task Table for Airplane Single-Engine Land updated
- Additional Rating Task Table for Airplane Single-Engine Sea updated
- Judgment Assessment Matrix
- Areas of Operation, updated

  o I. Preflight Preparation

    - Task C, Weather Information
    - Task D, Cross Country Flight Planning
    - Task E, National Airspace System

  o II. Preflight Procedures

- Task E, Taxiing and Sailing
- Task D, Taxiing
- Task F, Runway Incursion Avoidance
- Task G, Before Takeoff Check

o III. Airport and Seaplane Base Operations

- Task A, Radio Communication and ATC Light Signals
- Task B, Traffic Patterns

o IV. Takeoffs, Landings, and Go-Arounds

NOTE: *Added Runway Incursion Avoidance to ASEL Tasks.*

- Task A, Normal and Crosswind Takeoff and Climb
- Task B, Normal and Crosswind Approach and Landing
- Task C, Soft-Field Takeoff and Climb
- Task D, Soft-Field Approach and Landing
- Task E, Short-Field Takeoff and Maximum Performance Climb
- Task F, Short-Field Approach and Landing
- Task G, Glassy Water Takeoff and Climb
- Task H, Glassy Water Approach and Landing
- Task I, Rough Water Takeoff and Climb
- Task J, Rough Water Approach and Landing
- Task K, Forward Slip to a Landing
- Task L, Power-Off 180° Accuracy Approach and Landing
- Task M, Go-Around/Rejected Landing

o V. Performance Maneuvers

- Task B, Steep Spiral

o VI. Ground Reference Maneuver
o VII. Navigation

- Task B, Pilotage and Dead Reckoning

o VIII. Slow Flight and Stalls

- Note added

o IX. Emergency Operations

- Task A, Emergency Descent
- Task C, Systems and Equipment Malfunctions

Section 2, Commercial Pilot—Airplane (Multiengine Land and Multiengine Sea)

- Additional Rating Task Table for Airplane Multiengine Land updated
- Additional Rating Task Table for Airplane Multiengine Sea updated
- Judgment Assessment Matrix
- Areas of Operation, updated

  o I. Preflight Preparation

    - Task C, Weather Information
    - Task D, Cross Country Flight Planning
    - Task E, National Airspace System
    - Task K, Aeromedical Factors

  o II. Preflight Procedures

    - Task D, Taxiing
    - Task F, Runway Incursion Avoidance
    - Task G, Before Takeoff Check

  o III. Airport and Seaplane Base Operations

    - Task A, Radio Communication and ATC Light Signals

  o IV. Takeoffs, Landings, Stop and Go Landings, and Go-Arounds

NOTE: *Added Runway Incursion Avoidance to AMEL Tasks.*

    - Task A, Normal and Crosswind Takeoff and Climb
    - Task B, Normal and Crosswind Approach and Landing
    - Task C, Short-Field Takeoff and Maximum Performance Climb
    - Task D, Short-Field Approach and Landing
    - Task E, Glassy Water Approach and Landing
    - Task F, Rough Water Takeoff and Climb
    - Task G, Rough Water Approach and Landing
    - Task H, Go-Around/Rejected Landing

- VI. Navigation

  - Task A, Pilotage and Dead Reckoning

- VII. Slow Flight and Stalls

  - Task C, Takeoff and Departure Stalls
  - Task D, Accelerated Stalls

- VIII. Emergency Operations

  - Note Added
  - Task C, Engine Failure After Lift-Off
  - Task E, Systems and Equipment Malfunctions

- X. Multiengine Operations

  - Notes added
  - Task B, V_{MC} Demonstration
  - Task D, Instrument Approach—One Engine Inoperative

Table of Contents

Introduction

Section 1: Commercial Pilot Airplane— Single-Engine Land and Single-Engine Sea

Areas of Operation:

Introduction

General Information

The Flight Standards Service of the Federal Aviation Administration (FAA) has developed this practical test as the standard that shall be used by FAA examiners[1] when conducting commercial pilot—airplane practical tests. Instructors are expected to use this practical test standard (PTS) when preparing applicants for practical tests. Applicants should be familiar with this PTS and refer to these standards during their training.

Information considered directive in nature is described in this PTS in terms, such as "shall" and "must" indicating the actions are mandatory. Guidance information is described in terms, such as "should" and "may" indicating the actions are desirable or permissive, but not mandatory.

The FAA gratefully acknowledges the valuable assistance provided by many individuals and organizations throughout the aviation community who contributed their time and talent in assisting with the revision of these practical test standards.

This PTS may be purchased from the Superintendent of Documents, U.S. Government Printing Office (GPO), Washington, DC 20402-9325, or from http://bookstore.gpo.gov. This PTS is also available for download, in pdf format, from www.faa.gov.

This PTS is published by the U.S. Department of Transportation, Federal Aviation Administration, Airman Testing Standards Branch, AFS-630, P.O. Box 25082, Oklahoma City, OK 73125. Comments regarding this handbook should be sent, in e-mail form, to AFS630comments@faa.gov.

Practical Test Standards Concept

Title 14 of the Code of Federal Regulations (14 CFR) part 61 specifies the areas in which knowledge and skill must be demonstrated by the applicant before the issuance of a commercial pilot certificate or rating. The CFRs provide the flexibility to permit the FAA to publish practical test standards containing the Areas of Operation and specific Tasks in which pilot competency shall be

---

[1] *The word "examiner" denotes either the FAA inspector, FAA designated pilot examiner, or other authorized person who conducts the practical test.*[1]

demonstrated. The FAA will revise this PTS whenever it is determined that changes are needed in the interest of safety. **Adherence to the provisions of the regulations and the practical test standards is mandatory for the evaluation of commercial pilot applicants.**

Practical Test Book Description

This test book contains the following Commercial Pilot—Airplane Practical Test Standards:

> **Section 1:** Airplane—Single-Engine Land and Sea
> **Section 2:** Airplane—Multiengine Land and Sea

The Commercial Pilot—Airplane includes the Areas of Operation and Tasks for the issuance of an initial commercial pilot certificate and for the addition of category ratings and/or class ratings to that certificate.

Practical Test Standards Description

Areas of Operation are phases of the practical test arranged in a logical sequence within each standard. They begin with Preflight Preparation and end with Postflight Procedures. The examiner; however, **may conduct the practical test in any sequence that will result in a complete and efficient test; however, the ground portion of the practical test shall be accomplished before the flight portion.**

Tasks are titles of knowledge areas, flight procedures, or maneuvers appropriate to an Area of Operation. The abbreviation(s) within parentheses immediately following a Task refer to the category and/or class aircraft appropriate to that Task. The meaning of each abbreviation is as follows.

> **ASEL:** Airplane—Single-Engine Land
> **AMEL:** Airplane—Multiengine Land
> **ASES:** Airplane—Single-Engine Sea
> **AMES:** Airplane—Multiengine Sea

NOTE: *When administering a test based on sections 1 and 2 of this PTS, the Tasks appropriate to the class airplane (ASEL, ASES, AMEL, or AMES) used for the test shall be included in the plan of action. The absence of a class indicates the Task is for all classes.*

NOTE is used to emphasize special considerations required in the Area of Operation or Task.

Reference identifies the publication(s) that describe(s) the Task. Descriptions of Tasks are not included in these standards because this information can be found in the current issue of the listed reference. Publications other than those listed may be used for references if their content conveys substantially the same meaning as the referenced publications.

These practical test standards are based on the following references.

14 CFR part 39	Airworthiness Directives
14 CFR part 43	Maintenance, Preventive Maintenance, Rebuilding, and Alteration
14 CFR part 61	Certification: Pilots, Flight Instructors, and Ground Instructors
14 CFR part 91	General Operating and Flight Rules
14 CFR part 93	Special Air Traffic Rules
AC 00-6	Aviation Weather
AC 00-45	Aviation Weather Services
AC 61-65	Certification: Pilots and Flight Instructors
AC 61-67	Stall and Spin Awareness Training
AC 91-73	Part 91 and 135 Single-Pilot Procedures During Taxi Operations
AC 61-84	Role of Preflight Preparation
AC 90-48	Pilots' Role in Collision Avoidance
AC 90-66	Recommended Standard Traffic Patterns and Practices for Aeronautical Operations at Airports Without Operating Control Towers
AC 91-69	Cold Weather Operation of Aircraft
AC 91-55	Reduction of Electrical System Failures Following Aircraft Engine Starting
AC 91-69	Seaplane Safety for FAR Part 91 Operations
AC 120-51	Crew Resource Management Training
AC 120-74	Parts 91, 121, 125 and 135 Flightcrew Procedures During Taxi Operations
AC 150-5340-18	Standards for Airport Sign Systems
AIM	Aeronautical Information Manual
A/FD	Airport/Facility Directory
FAA-H-8083-1	Aircraft Weight and Balance Handbook
FAA-H-8083-2	Risk Management Handbook
FAA-H-8083-3	Airplane Flying Handbook
FAA-H-8083-6	Advanced Avionics Handbook
FAA-H-8083-15	Instrument Flying Handbook

FAA-H-8083-23	Seaplane, Skiplane, and Float/Ski Equipped Helicopter Operations Handbook
FAA-H-8083-25	Pilot's Handbook of Aeronautical Knowledge
FAA-P-8740-19	Flying Light Twins Safely
NOTAMs	Notices to Airmen
POH/AFM	Pilot Operating Handbook FAA-Approved Flight Manual
Other	Navigation Charts
	Navigation Equipment Operation Manuals
	Seaplane Supplement
	USCG Navigation Rules, International–Inland

The Objective lists the elements that must be satisfactorily performed to demonstrate competency in a Task. The Objective includes:

1. specifically what the applicant should be able to do;
2. conditions under which the Task is to be performed; and
3. acceptable performance standards.

Abbreviations

14 CFR	Title 14 of the Code of Federal Regulations
AC	Advisory Circular
ADM	Aeronautical Decision-Making
AGL	Above Ground Level
AMEL	Airplane Multiengine Land
AMES	Airplane Multiengine Sea
ATC	Air Traffic Control
CDL	Configuration Deviation List
CFIT	Controlled Flight Into Terrain
CRM	Crew Resource Management
DA	Decision Altitude
DH	Decision Height
DP	Departure Procedure
FAA	Federal Aviation Administration
FAF	Final Approach Fix
FDC	Flight Data Center
FE	Flight Engineer
FMS	Flight Management System
FMSP	Flight Management System Procedures
FSB	Flight Standardization Board
FSD	Flight Simulation Device

FSDO	Flight Standards District Office
FTD	Flight Training Device
GLS	GNSS Landing System
GNSS	Global Navigation Satellite System
GPO	Government Printing Office
GPS	Global Positioning System
IAP	Instrument Approach Procedure
IFR	Instrument Flight Rules
ILS	Instrument Landing System
INS	Inertial Navigation System
LAHSO	Land and Hold Short Operations
LDA	Localizer-Type Directional Aid
LOC	ILS Localizer
MDA	Minimum Descent Altitude
MEL	Minimum Equipment List
NAVAID	Navigation Aid
NDB	Non-Directional Beacon
NOTAM	Notice to Airman
NWS	National Weather Service
POH	Pilot's Operating Handbook
PT	Procedure Turn
PTS	Practical Test Standard
RNAV	Area Navigation
SRM	Single-Pilot Resource Management
STAR	Standard Terminal Arrival
TAA	Terminal Arrival Area
$\mathbf{V_1}$	Takeoff Decision Speed
$\mathbf{V_2}$	Takeoff Safety Speed
VDP	Visual Descent Point
VFR	Visual Flight Rules
$\mathbf{V_{MC}}$	Minimum Control Speed with Critical Engine Inoperative
VMC	Visual Meteorological Conditions
VOR	Very High Frequency Omnidirectional Range
$\mathbf{V_R}$	Rotation Speed
$\mathbf{V_{REF}}$	Reference Landing Approach Speed
$\mathbf{V_{SSE}}$	Safe, Intentional, One-Engine Inoperative Speed
$\mathbf{V_X}$	Best Angle of Climb Speed
$\mathbf{V_Y}$	Best Rate of Climb Speed

Use of the Practical Test Standards

The FAA requires that all commercial pilot practical tests be conducted in accordance with the appropriate commercial practical test standards and the policies set forth in the INTRODUCTION. Applicants shall be evaluated in **ALL** Tasks included in each Area of Operation of the appropriate practical test standard, unless otherwise noted.

An applicant, who holds at least a commercial pilot certificate seeking an additional airplane category rating and/or class rating at the private pilot level, shall be evaluated in the Areas of Operation and Tasks listed in the Additional Rating Task Table. At the discretion of the examiner, an evaluation of the applicant's competence in the remaining Areas of Operation and Tasks may be conducted.

If the applicant holds two or more category or class ratings at least at the commercial level, and the ratings table indicates differing required Tasks, the "least restrictive" entry applies. For example, if "ALL" and "NONE" are indicated for one Area of Operation, the "NONE" entry applies. If "B" and "B, C" are indicated, the "B" entry applies.

In preparation for each practical test, the examiner shall develop a written "plan of action" for each practical test. The "plan of action" is a tool, for the sole use of the examiner, to be used in evaluating the applicant. The plan of action need not be grammatically correct or in any formal format. The plan of action must contain all of the required Areas of Operation and Tasks and any optional Tasks selected by the examiner. The plan of action will include a scenario that allows the evaluation of as many required Areas of Operation and Tasks as possible without disruption. During the mission, the examiner interjects problems and emergencies which the applicant must manage. It should be structured so that most of the Areas of Operation and Tasks are accomplished within the mission. The examiner is afforded the flexibility to change the plan to accommodate unexpected situations as they arise. Some tasks (e.g., unusual attitudes) are not normally done during routine flight operations or may not fit into the scenario.

These maneuvers still must be demonstrated. It is preferable that these maneuvers be demonstrated after the scenario is completed. A practical test scenario can be suspended to do maneuvers, and then resumed if time and efficiency of the practical test so dictates. *Any Task selected for evaluation during a practical test shall be evaluated in its entirety.*

The examiner is expected to use good judgment in the performance of simulated emergency procedures. The use of the safest means for simulation is expected. Consideration must be given to local conditions, both meteorological and topographical, at the time of the test, as well as the applicant's workload, and the condition of the aircraft used. If the procedure being evaluated would jeopardize safety, it is expected that the applicant will simulate that portion of the maneuver.

Special Emphasis Areas

Examiners shall place special emphasis upon areas of aircraft operations considered critical to flight safety. Among these are:

1. Positive aircraft control,
2. Positive exchange of the flight controls procedure,
3. Stall/spin awareness,
4. Collision avoidance,
5. Wake turbulence avoidance,
6. LAHSO,
7. Runway incursion avoidance,
8. CFIT,
9. ADM and risk management,
10. Wire strike avoidance,
11. Checklist usage,
12. Temporary flight restrictions (TFRs),
13. Special use airspace (SUA),
14. Aviation security,
15. Single-Pilot Resource Management (SRM), and
16. Other areas deemed appropriate to any phase of the practical test.

A given special emphasis area may not be specifically addressed under a given Task. All areas are essential to flight and will be evaluated during the practice test.

Removal of the "Airplane Multiengine VFR Only" Limitation

The removal of the "Airplane Multiengine VFR Only" limitation, at the commercial pilot certificate level, requires an applicant to satisfactorily perform the following Area of Operation and Tasks from the commercial AMEL and AMES PTS in a multiengine airplane that has a manufacturer's published V_{MC} speed.

- Area of Operation X: Multiengine Operations

  o Task C: Engine Failure During Flight (By Reference to Instruments) o Task D: Instrument Approach—One Engine Inoperative (By Reference to Instruments)

Removal of the "Limited to Center Thrust" Limitation

The removal of the "Limited to Center Thrust" limitation at the commercial pilot certificate level requires an applicant to satisfactorily perform the following Areas of Operation and Tasks from the commercial AMEL and AMES PTS in a multiengine airplane that has a manufacturer's published V_{MC} speed. An applicant that holds an airplane instrument rating and has not demonstrated instrument proficiency in a multiengine airplane with a published V_{MC} shall complete the additional Tasks listed under Removal of the "Airplane Multiengine VFR Only" Limitation section.

▪ Area of Operation I: Preflight Preparation

 o Task H: Principles of Flight-Engine Inoperative

▪ Area of Operation IX: Emergency Operations

 o Task B: Engine Failure During Takeoff Before V_{MC} (Simulated)
 o Task C: Engine Failure After Lift-Off (Simulated)
 o Task D: Approach and Landing with an Inoperative Engine (Simulated)

▪ Area of Operation XI: Multiengine Operations

 o Task A: Maneuvering with One Engine Inoperative
 o Task B: V_{MC} Demonstration

Commercial Pilot – Airplane Practical Test Prerequisites

An applicant for the Commercial Pilot—Airplane Practical Test is required by 14 CFR part 61 to:

1. be at least 18 years of age;
2. be able to read, speak, write, and understand the English language. If there is a doubt, use AC 60-28, English Language Skill Standards;
3. possess a private pilot certificate if a commercial pilot certificate with an airplane rating is sought, or meet the flight experience required for a private pilot certificate (airplane rating) and pass the private airplane knowledge and practical test;

4. possess an instrument rating (airplane) or the following limitation shall be placed on the commercial pilot certificate: "Carrying passengers in airplanes for hire is prohibited at night or on cross-country flights of more than 50 nautical miles;"
5. have passed the appropriate commercial pilot knowledge test since the beginning of the 24th month before the month in which he or she takes the practical test;
6. have satisfactorily accomplished the required training and obtained the aeronautical experience prescribed;
7. possess at least a current third class medical certificate or, when a military pilot of the U.S. Armed Forces, can show and present evidence of an up-to-date medical examination authorizing pilot status issued by the U.S. Armed Forces;
8. receive and log ground training from an authorized instructor or complete a home-study course on the aeronautical knowledge areas of 14 CFR part 61.125 paragraph (b) that apply to the aircraft category and class rating sought; and; have an endorsement from an authorized instructor certifying that the applicant has received and logged training time within 2 calendar months preceding the date of application in preparation for the practical test and is prepared for the practical test;
9. also have an endorsement certifying that the applicant has demonstrated satisfactory knowledge of the subject areas in which the applicant was deficient on the airman knowledge test. (not required for power aircraft to power aircraft for additional category or class rating)

Aircraft and Equipment Required for the Practical Test

The commercial pilot—airplane applicant is required by 14 CFR section 61.45 to provide an airworthy, certificated aircraft for use during the practical test. This section further requires that the aircraft must:

1. be of U.S., foreign, or military registry of the same category, class, and type, if applicable, for the certificate and/or rating for which the applicant is applying;
2. have fully functioning dual controls, except as provided for in 14 CFR section 61.45(c) and (e);
3. be capable of performing all Areas of Operation appropriate to the rating sought and have no operating limitations which prohibit its use in any of the Areas of Operation required for the practical test; and
4. be a complex airplane furnished by the applicant, unless the applicant currently holds a commercial pilot certificate

with a single-engine or multiengine class rating as appropriate, for the performance of takeoffs, landings, and appropriate emergency procedures. A complex landplane is one having retractable landing gear, flaps, and controllable propeller or turbine-powered. A complex seaplane is one having flaps and controllable propeller.

Use of FAA-Approved Flight Simulation Training Device (FSTD)

An airman applicant for Commercial Pilot-Airplane Certification is authorized to use a full flight simulator (FFS) qualified by the National Simulator Program as levels A–D and/or a flight training device (FTD) qualified by the National Simulator Program as levels 4–7 to complete certain flight Task requirements listed in this practical test standard.

In order to do so, such devices must be used pursuant to and in accordance with a curriculum approved for use at a 14 CFR part 141 pilot school or 14 CFR part 142 training center. Practical tests or portions thereof, when accomplished in an FSTD may only be conducted by FAA aviation safety inspectors, designees authorized to conduct such tests in FSTDs for part 141 pilot school graduates, or appropriately authorized part 142 Training Center Evaluators (TCE).

When flight Tasks are accomplished in an aircraft, certain Task elements may be accomplished through "simulated" actions in the interest of safety and practicality, but when accomplished in a flight simulator or flight or flight training device, these same actions would not be "simulated." For example, when in an aircraft, a simulated engine fire may be addressed by retarding the throttle to idle, simulating the shutdown of the engine, simulating the discharge of the fire suppression agent, if applicable, simulating the disconnection of associated electrical, hydraulic, and pneumatics systems. However, when the same emergency condition is addressed in a FSTD, all Task elements must be accomplished as would be expected under actual circumstances.

Similarly, safety of flight precautions taken in the aircraft for the accomplishment of a specific maneuver or procedure (such as limiting altitude in an approach to stall or setting maximum airspeed for an engine failure expected to result in a rejected takeoff) need not be taken when a FSTD is used.

It is important to understand that, whether accomplished in an aircraft or FSTD, all Tasks and elements for each maneuver or procedure shall have the same performance standards applied equally for determination of overall satisfactory performance.

Training devices other than Flight Simulation Training Devices (FSTDs) may be used IAW AC-61-136.

Flight Instructor Responsibility

An appropriately rated flight instructor is responsible for training the commercial pilot applicant to acceptable standards in all subject matter areas, procedures, and maneuvers included in the Tasks within each Area of Operation in the appropriate commercial pilot practical test standard, even if the applicant is adding a category or class rating.

Because of the impact of their teaching activities in developing safe, proficient pilots, flight instructors should exhibit a high level of knowledge, skill, and the ability to impart that knowledge and skill to students.

Throughout the applicant's training, the flight instructor is responsible for emphasizing the performance of effective visual scanning and collision avoidance procedures, and the manufactures recommended procedures for the airplane flown and other areas deemed appropriate to the practical test.

Examiner Responsibility

The examiner conducting the practical test is responsible for determining that the applicant meets the acceptable standards of knowledge and skill of each Task within the appropriate practical test standard. Since there is no formal division between the "oral" and "skill" portions of the practical test, this becomes an ongoing process throughout the test. Oral questioning, to determine the applicant's knowledge of Tasks and related safety factors, should be used judiciously at all times, especially during the flight portion of the practical test. Examiners shall test to the greatest extent practicable the applicant's correlative abilities rather than mere rote enumeration of facts throughout the practical test.

If the examiner determines that a Task is incomplete, or the outcome uncertain, the examiner may require the applicant to repeat that Task, or portions of that Task. This provision has been made in the interest of fairness and does not mean that instruction, practice, or the repeating of an unsatisfactory task is permitted during the certification process. When practical, the remaining Tasks of the practical test phase should be completed before repeating the questionable Task.

On multiengine practical tests, where the failure of the most critical engine after lift off is required, the examiner must give consideration to local atmospheric conditions, terrain, and type of aircraft used. However, the failure of an engine shall not be simulated until attaining at least $V_{SSE}/V_{XSE}/V_{YSE}$ and at an altitude not lower than 500 feet AGL.

During simulated engine failures on multiengine practical tests, the examiner shall set zero thrust after the applicant has simulated feathering the propeller. The examiner shall require the applicant to demonstrate at least one landing with a simulated feathered propeller with the engine set to zero thrust. The feathering of one propeller shall be demonstrated in flight, unless the manufacturer prohibits the intentional feathering of the propellers during flight.

Throughout the flight portion of the practical test, the examiner shall evaluate the applicant's use of visual scanning and collision avoidance procedures.

Satisfactory Performance

Satisfactory performance to meet the requirements for certification is based on the applicant's ability to safely:

1. perform the Tasks specified in the Areas of Operation for the certificate or rating sought within the approved standards;
2. demonstrate mastery of the aircraft by performing each task successfully;
3. demonstrate satisfactory proficiency and competency within the approved standards;
4. demonstrate sound judgment and exercises aeronautical decision-making/risk management; and
5. demonstrate single-pilot competence if the aircraft is type certificated for single-pilot operations.

If the applicant satisfactorily performs the five items listed above, FAA Form 8060-4, Temporary Airman Certificate, or the appropriate IACRA form will be issued.

Unsatisfactory Performance

The tolerances represent the performance expected in good flying conditions. If, in the judgment of the examiner, the applicant does not meet the standards of performance of any Task performed, the associated Area of Operation is failed and therefore, the practical test is failed.

The examiner or applicant may discontinue the test at any time when the failure of an Area of Operation makes the applicant ineligible for the certificate or rating sought. The test may be continued ONLY with the consent of the applicant. If the test is discontinued, the applicant is entitled credit for only those Areas of Operation and their associated Tasks satisfactorily performed. However, during the retest, and at the discretion of the examiner, any Task may be reevaluated, including those previously passed.

Typical areas of unsatisfactory performance and grounds for disqualification are:

1. Any action or lack of action by the applicant that requires corrective intervention by the examiner to maintain safe flight.
2. Failure to use proper and effective visual scanning techniques to clear the area before and while performing maneuvers.
3. Consistently exceeding tolerances stated in the Objectives.
4. Failure to take prompt corrective action when tolerances are exceeded.

When a notice of disapproval is issued, the examiner shall record the applicant's unsatisfactory performance in terms of the Area of Operation and specific Task(s) not meeting the standard appropriate to practical test conducted. The AREA(s) OF OPERATION/Task(s) not tested and the number of practical test failures shall also be recorded. If the applicant fails the practical test because of a special emphasis area, the Notice of Disapproval shall indicate the associated task. i.e.: Area of Operation VIII, Maneuvering During Slow Flight, failure to use proper collision avoidance procedures.

Letter of Discontinuance

When a practical test is discontinued for reasons other than unsatisfactory performance (i.e., equipment failure, weather, illness), the FAA Form 8710-1, Airman Certificate and/or Rating Application, and, if applicable, the Airman Knowledge Test Report, is returned to the applicant. The examiner then must prepare, sign, and issue a Letter of Discontinuance to the applicant. The Letter of Discontinuance must identify the Areas of Operation and the associated Tasks of the practical test that were successfully completed. The applicant must be advised that the Letter of Discontinuance must be presented to the examiner, to receive credit for the items successfully completed, when the practical test is resumed, and made part of the certification file.

Single-Pilot Resource Management (SRM)

The examiner shall evaluate the applicant's ability throughout the practical test to use good aeronautical decision-making procedures in order to evaluate risks. The examiner shall accomplish this requirement by developing a scenario that incorporates as many Tasks as possible to evaluate the applicants risk management in making safe aeronautical decisions. For example, the examiner may develop a scenario that incorporates weather decisions and performance planning.

The applicant's ability to utilize all the assets available in making a risk analysis to determine the safest course of action is essential for satisfactory performance. The scenario should be realistic and within the capabilities of the aircraft used for the practical test.

Single-Pilot Resource Management (SRM) is defined as the art and science of managing all the resources (both onboard the aircraft and from outside sources) available to a single-pilot (prior and during flight) to ensure that the successful outcome of the flight is never in doubt. SRM available resources can include human resources, hardware, and information. Human resources ". . . includes all other groups routinely working with the pilot who are involved in decisions that are required to operate a flight safely. These groups include, but are not limited to: dispatchers, weather briefers, maintenance personnel, and air traffic controllers." SRM is a set of skill competencies that must be evident in all Tasks in this practical test standard as applied to single-pilot operation.

The following six items are areas of SRM:

- **Aeronautical Decision-Making**

References: *FAA-H-8083-15, FAA-H-8083-25; AC 60-22.*

Objective: To determine that the applicant exhibits sound aeronautical decision-making during the planning and execution of the planned flight. The applicant should:

1. Use a sound decision-making process, such as the DECIDE model, 3P model, or similar process when making critical decisions that will have an effect on the outcome of the flight. The applicant should be able to explain the factors and alternative courses of action that were considered while making the decision.
2. Recognize and explain any hazardous attitudes that may have influenced any decision.
3. Decide and execute an appropriate course of action to properly handle any situation that arises that may cause a

change in the original flight plan in such a way that leads to a safe and successful conclusion of the flight.

4. Explain how the elements of risk management, CFIT awareness, overall situational awareness, use of automation, and task management influenced the decisions made and the resulting course of action.

▪ **Risk Management:**

References: *FAA-H-8083-25, FITS document, Managing Risk through Scenario Based Training, Single-Pilot Resource Management, and Learner Centered Grading.*

Objective: To determine that the applicant can utilize risk management tools and models to assess the potential risk associated with the planned flight during preflight planning and while in flight. The applicant should:

1. Explain the four fundamental risk elements associated with the flight being conducted in the given scenario and how each one was assessed.
2. Use a tool, such as the PAVE checklist, to help assess the four risk elements.
3. Use a personal checklist, such as the I'MSAFE checklist, to determine personal risks.
4. Use weather reports and forecasts to determine weather risks associated with the flight.
5. Explain how to recognize risks and how to mitigate those risks throughout the flight.
6. Use the 5P model to assess the risks associated with each of the five factors.

▪ **Task Management**

Reference: *FAA-H-8083-15.*

Objective: To determine that the applicant can prioritize the various tasks associated with the planning and execution of the flight. The applicant should:

1. Explain how to prioritize tasks in such a way to minimize distractions from flying the aircraft.
2. Complete all tasks in a timely manner considering the phase of flight without causing a distraction from flying.
3. Execute all checklists and procedures in a manner that does not increase workload at critical times.

- **Situational Awareness**

References: FAA-H-8083-15, FAA-H-8083-25.

Objective: To determine that the applicant can maintain situational awareness during all phases of the flight. The applicant should:

1. Explain the concept of situational awareness and associated factors.
2. Explain the dangers associated with becoming fixated on a particular problem to the exclusion of other aspects of the flight.
3. State the current situation at any time during the flight in such a way that displays an accurate assessment of the current and future status of the flight, including weather, terrain, traffic, ATC situation, fuel status, and aircraft status.
4. Explain taxi operation planning procedures, such as recording taxi instructions, reading back taxi clearances, and reviewing taxi routes on the airport diagram.
5. Explain procedures for steering, maneuvering, maintaining taxi, runway position, and situational awareness.
6. Explain procedures for holding the pilot's workload to a minimum during taxi operations which should increase the pilot's awareness during taxiing.
7. ATC communications and pilot operations before takeoff, before landing, and after landing at controlled and uncontrolled airports.
8. Uses the navigation displays, traffic displays, terrain displays, weather displays, and other features of the aircraft to maintain a complete and accurate awareness of the current situation and any reasonably anticipated changes that may occur.

- **Controlled Flight Into Terrain Awareness**

References: Controlled Flight Into Terrain Training Aid website: http://www.faa.gov/training_testing/training/media/cfit/volume1/titlepg.pdf.

Objective: To determine that the applicant can accurately assess risks associated with terrain and obstacles, maintain accurate awareness of terrain and obstacles, and can use appropriate techniques and procedures to avoid controlled flight into terrain or obstacles by using all resources available. The applicant should:

1. Use current charts and procedures during the planning of the flight to ensure the intended flight path avoids terrain and obstacles.
2. Be aware of potential terrain and obstacle hazards along the intended route.
3. Explain the terrain display, TAWS, and/or GPWS as installed in the aircraft.
4. Use the terrain display, TAWS, and/or GPWS of the navigation displays as appropriate to maintain awareness and to avoid terrain and obstacles.
5. Plan departures and arrivals to avoid terrain and obstacles.
6. Alter flight as necessary to avoid terrain.
7. Plan any course diversion, for whatever reason, in such a way to ensure proper terrain and obstruction clearance to the new destination.
8. Explain and understand aircraft performance limitations associated with CFIT accidents.

- **Automation Management**

References: FAA-H-8083-6, FAA-8083-15.

Objective: To determine that the applicant can effectively use the automation features of the aircraft, including autopilot and flight management systems, in such a way to manage workload and can remain aware of the current and anticipated modes and status of the automation. The applicant should:

1. Explain how to recognize the current mode of operation of the autopilot/FMS.
2. Explain how to recognize anticipated and unanticipated mode or status changes of the autopilot/FMS.
3. State at any time during the flight the current mode or status and what the next anticipated mode or status will be.
4. Use the autopilot/FMS to reduce workload as appropriate for the phase of flight, during emergency or abnormal operations.
5. Recognize unanticipated mode changes in a timely manner and promptly return the automation to the correct mode.

Applicant's Use of Checklists

Throughout the practical test, the applicant is evaluated on the use of an approved manufacturer's checklist or equivalent. If no manufacturer's checklist is published, the appropriate FAA Handbook or equivalent checklist maybe used. Proper use is dependent on the specific Task being evaluated. The situation may be such that the use of the checklist, while accomplishing elements of an Objective, would be either unsafe or impractical, especially in a single-pilot operation. In this case, a review of the checklist after the elements have been accomplished would be appropriate. Division of attention and proper visual scanning should be considered when using a checklist.

Use of Distractions During Practical Tests

Numerous studies indicate that many accidents have occurred when the pilot has been distracted during critical phases of flight. To evaluate the applicant's ability to utilize proper control technique while dividing attention both inside and/or outside the cockpit, the examiner shall cause realistic distractions during the flight portion of the practical test to evaluate the applicant's ability to divide attention while maintaining safe flight.

Positive Exchange of Flight Controls

During flight training, there must always be a clear understanding between students and flight instructors of who has control of the aircraft. Prior to flight, a briefing should be conducted that includes the procedure for the exchange of flight controls. A positive three-step process in the exchange of flight controls between pilots is a proven procedure and one that is strongly recommended.

When the instructor wishes the student to take control of the aircraft, he or she will say, "You have the flight controls." The student acknowledges immediately by saying, "I have the flight controls." The flight instructor again says, "You have the flight controls." When control is returned to the instructor, follow the same procedure. A visual check is recommended to verify that the exchange has occurred. There should never by any doubt as to who is flying the aircraft.

Stalls and Spin Awareness

During flight training, there must always be a clear understanding concerning stalls and spin awareness. All stalls at the commercial level will be in accordance with FAA policy. All stalls will be recovered no lower than 1,500 feet AGL for single-engine airplanes; 3,000 feet AGL for multiengine airplanes, unless the manufacturer recommends a higher altitude to initiate the recovery.

Section 1:

Commercial Pilot Airplane—

Single-Engine Land

and

Single-Engine Sea

(this page intentionally left blank)

Additional Rating Task Table:

Airplane Single-Engine Land

Addition of an Airplane Single-Engine Land Rating to an existing Commercial Pilot Certificate
Required Tasks are indicated by either the Task letter(s) that apply(s) or an indication that all or none of the Tasks must be tested based on the notes in each Area of Operation.

COMMERCIAL PILOT RATING(S) HELD

AREAS OF OPER-ATION	ASES	AMEL	AMES	RH	RG	Glider	Balloon	Airship
I	F,G	F,G	F,G	F,G	F,G	F,G	F,G	F,G
II	D,F	D,F	D,F	A,C,D, F,G	A,D,F, G	A,B,C, D,F,G	A,B,C, D,F,G	A,B,C, D,F,G
III	C	NONE	C	B,C	NONE	B,C	B,C	B,C
IV	A,B,C, D,E,F, K	A,B,C, D,E,F, K	A,B,C, D,E,F, K	A,B,C, D,E,F, K,L	A,B,C, D,E,F, K,L	A,B,C, D,E,F, K,L	A,B,C, D,E,F, K,L	A,B,C, D,E,F, K,L
V	NONE	B,C,D	B,C,D	ALL	ALL	ALL	ALL	ALL
VI	NONE	ALL	ALL	ALL	ALL	ALL	ALL	ALL
VII	NONE	NONE	NONE	NONE	NONE	ALL	ALL	NONE
VIII	NONE	NONE	NONE	ALL	ALL	ALL	ALL	ALL
IX	A,B,C	A,B,C	A,B,C	ALL	ALL	ALL	ALL	ALL
X	NONE	NONE	NONE	ALL	ALL	ALL	ALL	ALL
XI	A	NONE	A	A	A	A	A	A

Additional Rating Task Table:

Airplane Single-Engine Sea

Addition of an Airplane Single-Engine Sea Rating to an existing Commercial Pilot Certificate
Required Tasks are indicated by either the Task letter(s) that apply(s) or an indication that all or none of the Tasks must be tested based on the notes in each Area of Operation.

COMMERCIAL PILOT RATING(S) HELD

AREAS OF OPER-ATION	ASEL	AMEL	AMES	RH	RG	Glider	Balloon	Airship
I	F,G,H, I	F,G,H, I	F,G	F,G,H, I	F,G,H, I	F,G,H, I	F,G,H, I	F,G,H, I
II	E,F	E,F	E,F	A,B,C, E,F	A,B,E, F, G	A,B,C, E,F,G	A,B,C, E,F,G	A,B,C, E,F,G
III	C	C	NONE	B,C	C	B,C	B,C	B,C
IV	A,B,E, F,G,H, I,J	A,B,E, F,G,H, I,J	A,B,E, F,G,H, I,J	A,B,E, F,G,H, I,J,K,L	A,B,E, F,G,H, I,J,K,L	A,B,E, F,G,H, I,J,K,L	A,B,E, F,G,H, I,J,K,L	A,B,E, F,G,H, I,J,K,L
V	NONE	B,C,D	B,C,D	ALL	ALL	ALL	ALL	ALL
VI	NONE	ALL	ALL	ALL	ALL	ALL	ALL	ALL
VII	NONE	NONE	NONE	NONE	NONE	ALL	ALL	NONE
VIII	NONE	NONE	NONE	ALL	ALL	ALL	ALL	ALL
IX	A,B,C	A,B,C	A,B,C	ALL	ALL	ALL	ALL	ALL
X	NONE	NONE	NONE	ALL	ALL	ALL	ALL	ALL
XI	B,C,D	B,C,D	NONE	B,C,D	B,C,D	B,C,D	B,C,D	B,C,D

Applicant's Practical Test Checklist

Appointment with Examiner

Examiner's Name: _____

Location: _____

Date/Time: _____

ACCEPTABLE AIRCRAFT
- ☐ Aircraft Documents:
  - ☐ Airworthiness Certificate
  - ☐ Registration Certificate
  - ☐ Operating Limitations
- ☐ Aircraft Maintenance Records:
  - ☐ Logbook Record of Airworthiness Inspections and AD Compliance
- ☐ Pilot's Operating Handbook, FAA-Approved Airplane Flight Manual

PERSONAL EQUIPMENT
- ☐ View-Limiting Device
- ☐ Current Aeronautical Charts
- ☐ Computer and Plotter
- ☐ Flight Plan Form
- ☐ Flight Logs
- ☐ Current AIM, Airport Facility Directory, and Appropriate Publications

PERSONAL RECORDS
- ☐ Identification—Photo/Signature ID
- ☐ Pilot Certificate
- ☐ Current and Appropriate Medical Certificate
- ☐ Completed FAA Form 8710-1, Airman Certificate and/or Rating Application with Instructor's Signature (If applicable)
- ☐ Computer Test Report
- ☐ Pilot Logbook with appropriate Instructor Endorsements
- ☐ FAA Form 8060-5, Notice of Disapproval (if applicable)
- ☐ Approved School Graduation Certificate (if applicable)
- ☐ Examiner's Fee (if applicable)

(this page intentionally left blank)

Examiner's Practical Test Checklist

Airplane Single-Engine Land
and
Airplane Single-Engine Sea

Applicant's Name: _____

Location: _____

Date/Time: _____

I. PREFLIGHT PREPARATION
- ☐ A. Certificates and Documents (ASEL and ASES)
- ☐ B. Airworthiness Requirements (ASEL and ASES)
- ☐ C. Weather Information (ASEL and ASES)
- ☐ D. Cross-Country Flight Planning (ASEL and ASES)
- ☐ E. National Airspace System (ASEL and ASES)
- ☐ F. Performance and Limitations (ASEL and ASES)
- ☐ G. Operation of Systems (ASEL and ASES)
- ☐ H. Water and Seaplane Characteristics (ASES)
- ☐ I. Seaplane Bases, Maritime Rules, and Aids to Marine Navigation (ASES)
- ☐ J. Aeromedical Factors (ASEL and ASES)

II. PREFLIGHT PROCEDURES
- ☐ A. Preflight Inspection (ASEL and ASES)
- ☐ B. Cockpit Management (ASEL and ASES)
- ☐ C. Engine Starting (ASEL and ASES)
- ☐ D. Taxiing (ASEL)
- ☐ E. Taxiing and Sailing (ASES)
- ☐ F. Runway Incursion Avoidance (ASEL and AES)
- ☐ G. Before Takeoff Check (ASEL and ASES)

III. AIRPORT AND SEAPLANE BASE OPERATIONS
- ☐ A. Radio Communications and ATC Light Signals (ASEL and ASES)
- ☐ B. Traffic Patterns (ASEL and ASES)
- ☐ C. Airport/Seaplane Base, Runway, and Taxiway Signs, Markings, and Lighting (ASEL and ASES)

IV. TAKEOFFS, LANDINGS, AND GO-AROUNDS
- ☐ **A.** Normal and Crosswind Takeoff and Climb (ASEL and ASES)
- ☐ **B.** Normal and Crosswind Approach and Landing (ASEL and ASES)
- ☐ **C.** Soft-Field Takeoff and Climb (ASEL)
- ☐ **D.** Soft-Field Approach and Landing (ASEL)
- ☐ **E.** Short-Field (Confined Area—ASES) Takeoff and Maximum Performance Climb (ASEL and ASES)
- ☐ **F.** Short-Field Approach (Confined Area—ASES) and Landing (ASEL and ASES)
- ☐ **G.** Glassy Water Takeoff and Climb (ASES)
- ☐ **H.** Glassy Water Approach and Landing (ASES)
- ☐ **I.** Rough Water Takeoff and Climb (ASES)
- ☐ **J.** Rough Water Approach and Landing (ASES)
- ☐ **K.** Power-Off 180° Accuracy Approach and Landing (ASEL and ASES)
- ☐ **L.** Go-Around/Rejected Landing (ASEL and ASES)

V. PERFORMANCE MANEUVERS
- ☐ **A.** Steep Turns (ASEL and ASES)
- ☐ **B.** Steep Spiral (ASEL and ASES)
- ☐ **C.** Chandelles (ASEL and ASES)
- ☐ **D.** Lazy Eights (ASEL and ASES)

VI. GROUND REFERENCE MANEUVER
- ☐ **A.** Eights on Pylons (ASEL and ASES)

VII. NAVIGATION
- ☐ **A.** Pilotage and Dead Reckoning (ASEL and ASES)
- ☐ **B.** Navigation Systems and Radar Services (ASEL and ASES)
- ☐ **C.** Diversion (ASEL and ASES)
- ☐ **D.** Lost Procedures (ASEL and ASES)

VIII. SLOW FLIGHT AND STALLS
- ☐ **A.** Maneuvering During Slow Flight (ASEL and ASES)
- ☐ **B.** Power-Off Stalls (ASEL and ASES)
- ☐ **C.** Power-On Stalls (ASEL and ASES)
- ☐ **D.** Accelerated Stalls (ASEL and ASES)
- ☐ **E.** Spin Awareness (ASEL and ASES)

IX. EMERGENCY OPERATIONS

☐ **A.** Emergency Descents (ASEL and ASES)

☐ **B.** Emergency Approach and Landing (Simulated) (ASEL and ASES)

☐ **C.** Systems and Equipment Malfunctions (ASEL and ASES)

☐ **D.** Emergency Equipment and Survival Gear (ASEL and ASES)

X. HIGH ALTITUDE OPERATIONS

☐ **A.** Supplemental Oxygen (ASEL and ASES)

☐ **B.** Pressurization (ASEL and ASES)

XI. POSTFLIGHT PROCEDURES

☐ **A.** After Landing, Parking, and Securing (ASEL and ASES)

☐ **B.** Anchoring (ASES)

☐ **C.** Docking and Mooring (ASES)

☐ **D.** Ramping/Beaching (ASES)

(this page intentionally left blank)

(Change 1 – March 13, 2012: Judgment Assessment Matrix removed)

(this page intentionally left blank)

Areas of Operation:

I. Preflight Preparation

NOTE: The examiner shall develop a scenario based on real time weather to evaluate Tasks C and D.

Task A: Certificates and Documents (ASEL and ASES)

References: 14 CFR parts 39, 43, 61, 91; FAA-H-8083-3, FAA-H-8083-25; POH/AFM.

Objective: To determine that the applicant exhibits satisfactory knowledge of the elements related to certificates and documents by:

1. Explaining—

   a. commercial pilot certificate privileges, limitations, and recent flight experience requirements.
   b. medical certificate class and duration.
   c. pilot logbook or flight records.

2. Locating and explaining—

   a. airworthiness and registration certificates.
   b. operating limitations, placards, instrument markings, and POH/AFM.
   c. weight and balance data and equipment list.

Task B: Airworthiness Requirements (ASEL and ASES)

References: 14 CFR parts 39, 91; FAA-H-8083-25.

Objective: To determine that the applicant exhibits satisfactory knowledge of the elements related to airworthiness requirements by:

1. Explaining—

   a. required instruments and equipment for day/night VFR.
   b. procedures and limitations for determining airworthiness of the airplane with inoperative instruments and equipment with and without an MEL.

c. requirements and procedures for obtaining a special flight permit.

2. Locating and explaining—

a. airworthiness directives.
b. compliance records.
c. maintenance/inspection requirements.
d. appropriate record keeping.

Task C: Weather Information (ASEL and ASES)

References: 14 CFR part 91; AC 00-6, AC 00-45; AC 61-84; FAA-H-8083-25; AIM.

Objective: To determine that the applicant:

1. Exhibits satisfactory knowledge of the elements related to weather information by analyzing weather reports, charts, and forecasts from various sources with emphasis on—

a. METAR, TAF, and FA.
b. surface analysis chart.
c. radar summary chart.
d. winds and temperature aloft chart.
e. significant weather prognostic charts.
f. convective outlook chart.
g. AWOS, ASOS, and ATIS reports.
h. SIGMETs and AIRMETs.
i. PIREPs.
j. windshear reports.
k. icing and freezing level information.

2. Makes a competent "go/no-go" decision based on available weather information.

Task D: Cross-Country Flight Planning (ASEL and ASES)

References: 14 CFR part 91; FAA-H-8083-25; AC 61-84; Navigation Charts; AFD; AIM; NOTAMS.

Objective: To determine that the applicant:

1. Exhibits satisfactory knowledge of the elements related to cross-country flight planning by presenting and explaining a pre-planned VFR cross-country flight, as previously assigned by the examiner. On the day of the practical test,

the final flight plan shall be to the first fuel stop, based on maximum allowable passengers, baggage, and/or cargo loads using real-time weather.

2. Uses appropriate and current aeronautical charts.
3. Properly identifies airspace, obstructions, and terrain features.
4. Selects easily identifiable en route checkpoints.
5. Selects most favorable altitudes considering weather conditions and equipment capabilities.
6. Computes headings, flight time, and fuel requirements.
7. Selects appropriate navigation system/facilities and communication frequencies.
8. Applies pertinent information from AFD, NOTAMs, and NOTAMS relative to airport, runway and taxiway closures, and other flight publications.
9. Completes a navigation log and simulates filing a VFR flight plan.

Task E: National Airspace System (ASEL and ASES)

References: 14 CFR parts 71, 91, 93; Navigation Charts; AIM.

Objective: To determine that the applicant exhibits satisfactory knowledge of the elements related to the National Airspace System by explaining:

1. Basic VFR weather minimums—for all classes of airspace.
2. Airspace classes—their operating rules, pilot certification, and airplane equipment requirements for the following—

   a. Class A.
   b. Class B.
   c. Class C.
   d. Class D.
   e. Class E.
   f. Class G.

3. Special use, special flight rules areas, and other airspace areas.

Task F: Performance and Limitations (ASEL and ASES)

References: FAA-H-8083-1, FAA-H-8083-25; AC 61-84; POH/AFM.

Objective: To determine that the applicant:

1. Exhibits satisfactory knowledge of the elements related to performance and limitations by explaining the use of charts, tables, and data to determine performance and the adverse effects of exceeding limitations.
2. Computes weight and balance. Determines the computed weight and center of gravity are within the airplane's operating limitations and if the weight and center of gravity will remain within limits during all phases of flight.
3. Demonstrates use of the appropriate manufacturer's performance charts, tables, and data.
4. Describes the effects of atmospheric conditions on the airplane's performance.

Task G: Operation of Systems (ASEL and ASES)

References: FAA-H-8083-25, FAA-H-8083-23; POH/AFM.

Objective: To determine that the applicant exhibits satisfactory knowledge of the elements related to the operation of systems on the airplane provided for the flight test by explaining at least three of the following systems.

1. Primary flight controls and trim.
2. Flaps, leading edge devices, and spoilers.
3. Water rudders (ASES).
4. Powerplant and propeller.
5. Landing gear.
6. Fuel, oil, and hydraulic.
7. Electrical.
8. Avionics.
9. Pitot-static, vacuum/pressure, and associated flight instruments.
10. Environmental.
11. Deicing and anti-icing.

Task H: Water and Seaplane Characteristics (ASES)

Reference: FAA-H-8083-23.

Objective: To determine that the applicant exhibits satisfactory knowledge of the elements related to water and seaplane characteristics by explaining:

1. The characteristics of a water surface as affected by features, such as—

   a. size and location.

b. protected and unprotected areas.
c. surface wind.
d. direction and strength of water current.
e. floating and partially submerged debris.
f. sandbars, islands, and shoals.
g. vessel traffic and wakes.
h. other features peculiar to the area.

2. Float and hull construction, and their effect on seaplane performance.
3. Causes of porpoising and skipping, and the pilot action required to prevent or correct these occurrences.

Task I: Seaplane Bases, Maritime Rules, and Aids to Marine Navigation (ASES)

References: FAA-H-8083-23; AIM; USCG Navigation Rules; International–Inland; POH/AFM; AFD.

Objective: To determine that the applicant exhibits satisfactory knowledge of the elements related to seaplane bases, maritime rules, and aids to marine navigation by explaining:

1. How to locate and identify seaplane bases on charts or in directories.
2. Operating restrictions at various bases.
3. Right-of-way, steering, and sailing rules pertinent to seaplane operation.
4. Marine navigation aids, such as buoys, beacons, lights, and sound signals.

Task J: Aeromedical Factors (ASEL and ASES)

References: FAA-H-8083-25; AIM.

Objective: Satisfactory knowledge of the elements related to aeromedical factors by explaining:

1. The symptoms, causes, effects, and corrective actions of at least three of the following—

a. hypoxia.
b. hyperventilation.
c. middle ear and sinus problems.
d. spatial disorientation.
e. motion sickness.

f.   carbon monoxide poisoning.
g.   stress and fatigue.
h.   dehydration.

2. The effects of alcohol, drugs, and over-the-counter medications.
3. The effects of excess nitrogen during scuba dives upon a pilot or passenger in flight.

II. Preflight Procedures

Task A: Preflight Inspection (ASEL and ASES)

References: FAA-H-8083-3, FAA-H-8083-23; POH/AFM.

Objective: To determine that the applicant:

1. Exhibits satisfactory knowledge of the elements related to preflight inspection. This shall include which items must be inspected, the reasons for checking each item, and how to detect possible defects.
2. Inspects the airplane with reference to an appropriate checklist.
3. Verifies the airplane is in condition for safe flight.

Task B: Cockpit Management (ASEL and ASES)

References: FAA-H-8083-3; POH/AFM.

Objective: To determine that the applicant:

1. Exhibits satisfactory knowledge of the elements related to cockpit management procedures.
2. Ensures all loose items in the cockpit and cabin are secured.
3. Organizes material and equipment in an efficient manner so they are readily available.
4. Briefs occupants on the use of safety belts, shoulder harnesses, doors, and emergency procedures.

Task C: Engine Starting (ASEL and ASES)

References: FAA-H-8083-3, FAA-H-8083-23, FAA-H-8083-25; AC 91-13, AC 91-55; POH/AFM.

Objective: To determine that the applicant:

1. Exhibits satisfactory knowledge of the elements related to recommended engine starting procedures. This shall include the use of an external power source, hand propping safety, and starting under various atmospheric conditions.
2. Positions the airplane properly considering structures, surface conditions, other aircraft, and the safety of nearby persons and property.
3. Utilizes the appropriate checklist for starting procedure.

Task D: Taxiing (ASEL)

References: FAA-H-8083-3; POH/AFM.

Objective: To determine that the applicant:

1. Exhibits satisfactory knowledge of the elements related to safe taxi procedures at towered and non-towered airports.
2. Performs a brake check immediately after the airplane begins moving.
3. Positions the flight controls properly for the existing wind conditions.
4. Controls direction and speed without excessive use of brakes.
5. Exhibits procedures for steering, maneuvering, maintaining taxiway, runway position, and situational awareness to avoid runway incursions.
6. Exhibits proper positioning of the aircraft relative to hold lines.
7. Exhibits procedures to insure clearances/instructions are received and recorded/read back correctly.
8. Exhibits situational awareness/taxi procedures in the event the aircraft is on a taxiway that is between parallel runways.
9. Uses a taxi chart during taxi.
10. Complies with airport/taxiway markings, signals, ATC clearances, and instructions.
11. Utilizes procedures for eliminating pilot distractions.
12. Taxiing to avoid other aircraft/vehicles and hazards.

Task E: Taxiing and Sailing (ASES)

References: FAA-H-8083-23; USCG Navigation Rules; International–Inland; POH/AFM.

Objective: To determine that the applicant:

1. Exhibits satisfactory knowledge of the elements related to water taxi and sailing procedures.
2. Positions the flight controls properly for the existing wind conditions.
3. Plans and follows the most favorable course while taxiing or sailing. Considers wind, water current, water conditions, and maritime regulations, as appropriate.
4. Uses the appropriate idle, plow, or step taxi technique.
5. Uses flight controls, flaps, doors, water rudder, and power correctly so as to follow the desired course while sailing.
6. Prevents and corrects for porpoising and skipping.
7. Avoids other aircraft, vessels, and hazards.

8. Complies with seaplane base signs, signals, and clearances.

Task F: Runway Incursion Avoidance (ASEL and ASES)

References: FAA-H-8083-3, FAA-H-8083-25; AC 91-73, AC 150-5340-18; AIM.

Objective: To determine that the applicant exhibits knowledge of the elements of runway incursion avoidance by:

1. Exhibiting distinct challenges and requirements during taxi operations not found in other phases of flight operations.
2. Exhibiting procedures for appropriate cockpit activities during taxiing including taxi route planning, briefing the location of HOT SPOTS, communicating and coordinating with ATC.
3. Exhibiting procedures for steering, maneuvering, maintaining taxiway, runway position, and situational awareness.
4. Knowing the relevance/importance of hold lines.
5. Exhibiting procedures to ensure the pilot maintains strict focus to the movement of the aircraft and ATC communications, including the elimination of all distractive activities (i.e. cell phone, texting, conversations with passengers) during aircraft taxi, takeoff and climb out to cruise altitude.
6. Utilizing procedures for holding the pilot's workload to a minimum during taxi operations.
7. Utilizing taxi operation planning procedures, such as recording taxi instructions, reading back taxi clearances, and reviewing taxi routes on the airport diagram,
8. Utilizing procedures to insure that clearance or instructions that are actually received are adhered to rather than the ones expected to be received.
9. Utilizing procedures to maintain/enhance situational awareness when conducting taxi operations in relation to other aircraft operations in the vicinity as well as to other vehicles moving on the airport.
10. Exhibiting procedures for briefing if a landing rollout to a taxiway exit will place the pilot in close proximity to another runway which can result in a runway incursion.
11. Conducting appropriate after landing/taxi procedures in the event the aircraft is on a taxiway that is between parallel runways.
12. Knowing specific procedures for operations at an airport with an operating air traffic control tower, with emphasis on

ATC communications and runway entry/crossing authorizations.
13. Utilizing ATC communications and pilot actions before takeoff, before landing, and after landing at towered and non-towered airports.
14. Knowing procedures unique to night operations.
15. Knowing operations at non-towered airports.
16. Knowing the use of aircraft exterior lighting.
17. Knowing the hazards of Low visibility operations.

Task G: Before Takeoff Check (ASEL and ASES)

References: FAA-H-8083-3, FAA-H-8083-23; POH/AFM.

Objective: To determine that the applicant:

1. Exhibits satisfactory knowledge of the elements related to the before takeoff check. This shall include the reasons for checking each item and how to detect malfunctions.
2. Positions the airplane properly considering other aircraft/vessels, wind, and surface conditions.
3. Divides attention inside and outside the cockpit.
4. Ensures that engine temperature(s) and pressure(s) are suitable for runup and takeoff.
5. Accomplishes the before takeoff checklist and ensures the airplane is in safe operating condition as recommended by the manufacturer.
6. Reviews takeoff performance, such as airspeeds, takeoff distances, departure, and emergency procedures.
7. Avoids runway incursions and ensures no conflict with traffic prior to taxiing into takeoff position.

III. Airport and Seaplane Base Operations

Task A: *Radio Communications and ATC Light Signals (ASEL and ASES)*

References: 14 CFR part 91; FAA-H-8083-25; AIM.

Objective: To determine that the applicant:

1. Exhibits satisfactory knowledge of the elements related to radio communications and ATC light signals.
2. Selects appropriate frequencies.
3. Transmits using AIM specified phraseology and procedures.
4. Acknowledges radio communications and complies with instructions.

Task B: *Traffic Patterns (ASEL and ASES)*

References: FAA-H-8083-3, FAA-H-8083-25; AC 90-66; AIM.

Objective: To determine that the applicant:

1. Exhibits satisfactory knowledge of the elements related to traffic patterns. This shall include procedures at airports with and without operating control towers, prevention of runway incursions, collision avoidance, wake turbulence avoidance, and wind shear.
2. Properly identifies and interprets airport/seaplane base runways, taxiway signs, markings, and lighting.
3. Complies with proper traffic pattern procedures.
4. Maintains proper spacing from other aircraft.
5. Corrects for wind drift to maintain the proper ground track.
6. Maintains orientation with the runway/landing area in use.
7. Maintains traffic pattern altitude, ±100 feet, and the appropriate airspeed, ±10 knots.

Task C: *Airport/Seaplane Base, Runway, and Taxiway Signs, Markings, and Lighting (ASEL and ASES)*

References: FAA-H-8083-23, FAA-H-8083-25; AIM; AFD; AC 91-73, AC 150-5340-18.

Objective: To determine that the applicant:

1. Exhibits satisfactory knowledge of the elements related to airport/seaplane base, runway, and taxiway operations with emphasis on runway incursion avoidance.
2. Properly identifies and interprets airport/seaplane base, runway, and taxiway signs, markings, and lighting, with emphasis on runway incursion avoidance.

IV. Takeoffs, Landings, and Go-Arounds

Task A: *Normal and Crosswind Takeoff and Climb (ASEL and ASES)*

NOTE: *If a crosswind condition does not exist, the applicant's knowledge of crosswind elements shall be evaluated through oral testing.*

References: FAA-H-8083-3, FAA-H-8083-23; POH/AFM.

Objective: To determine that the applicant:

1. Utilizes procedures before taxiing onto the runway or takeoff area to ensure runway incursion avoidance. Verify ATC clearance/no aircraft on final at non-towered airports before entering the runway, and ensure that the aircraft is on the correct takeoff runway.
2. Exhibits satisfactory knowledge of the elements related to a normal and crosswind takeoff, climb operations, and rejected takeoff procedures.
3. Ascertains wind direction with or without visible wind direction indicators.
4. Calculates/determines if crosswind component is above his or her ability or that of the aircraft's capability.
5. Positions the flight controls for the existing wind conditions.
6. Clears the area, taxies onto the takeoff surface, and aligns the airplane on the runway center/takeoff path.
7. Retracts the water rudders as appropriate (ASES), and advances the throttle smoothly to takeoff power.
8. Establishes and maintains the most efficient planing/lift off attitude and corrects for porpoising and skipping (ASES).
9. Rotates and lifts off at the recommended airspeed and accelerates to V_Y.
10. Establishes a pitch attitude that will maintain $V_Y, \pm 5$ knots.
11. Retracts the landing gear, if appropriate, and flaps after a positive rate of climb is established.
12. Maintains takeoff power and $V_Y \pm 5$ knots to a safe maneuvering altitude.
13. Maintains directional control, proper wind-drift correction throughout the takeoff and climb.
14. Complies with responsible environmental practices, to include noise abatement procedures.
15. Completes appropriate checklists.

Task B: Normal and Crosswind Approach and Landing (ASEL and ASES)

NOTE: *If a crosswind condition does not exist, the applicant's knowledge of crosswind elements shall be evaluated through oral testing.*

References: FAA-H-8083-3, FAA-H-8083-23; POH/AFM.

Objective: To determine that the applicant:

1. Exhibits satisfactory knowledge of the elements related to a normal and crosswind approach and landing.
2. Adequately surveys the intended landing area (ASES).
3. Considers the wind conditions, landing surface, obstructions, and selects a suitable touchdown point.
4. Establishes the recommended approach and landing configuration and airspeed, and adjusts pitch attitude and power as required.
5. Maintains a stabilized approach and recommended airspeed or in its absence, not more than 1.3 V_{SO}, ±5 knots, with wind gust factor applied.
6. Makes smooth, timely, and correct control application during the round out and touchdown.
7. Contacts the water at the proper pitch attitude (ASES).
8. Touches down smoothly at approximate stalling speed (ASEL).
9. Touches down within the available runway, or water landing area, within 200 feet beyond a specified point with no drift, and with the airplane's longitudinal axis aligned with and over the runway center/landing path.
10. Maintains crosswind correction and directional control throughout the approach and landing sequence.
11. Executes a timely go-around decision when the approach cannot be made within the tolerance specified above.
12. Utilizes after landing runway incursion avoidance procedures.
13. Completes the appropriate checklist.

Task C: Soft-Field Takeoff and Climb (ASEL)

References: FAA-H-8083-3; POH/AFM.

Objective: To determine that the applicant:

1. Utilizes procedures before taxiing onto the runway or takeoff area to ensure runway incursion avoidance. Verify ATC clearance/no aircraft on final at non-towered airports

before entering the runway, and ensure that the aircraft is on the correct takeoff runway.

2. Exhibits satisfactory knowledge of the elements related to a soft-field takeoff and climb.
3. Positions the flight controls for existing conditions and to maximize lift as quickly as possible.
4. Clears the area; taxies onto takeoff surface at a speed consistent with safety and aligns the airplane without stopping while advancing the throttle smoothly to takeoff power.
5. Establishes and maintains a pitch attitude that will transfer the weight of the airplane from the wheels to the wings as rapidly as possible.
6. Rotates and lifts off at the lowest possible airspeed and remains in ground effect while accelerating to V_X or V_Y, as appropriate.
7. Establishes a pitch attitude for V_X or V_Y, as appropriate, and maintains selected airspeed ±5 knots during the climb.
8. Retracts the landing gear, if appropriate, and flaps after clear of any obstacles or as recommended by the manufacturer.
9. Maintains takeoff power and V_X or V_Y ±5 knots to a safe maneuvering altitude.
10. Maintains directional control and proper wind-drift correction throughout the takeoff and climb.
11. Completes appropriate checklist.

Task D: Soft-Field Approach and Landing (ASEL)

References: FAA-H-8083-3; POH/AFM.

Objective: To determine that the applicant:

1. Exhibits satisfactory knowledge of the elements related to a soft-field approach and landing.
2. Considers the wind conditions, landing surface, and obstructions, and selects the most suitable touchdown area.
3. Establishes the recommended approach and landing configuration and airspeed; adjusts pitch attitude and power as required.
4. Maintains a stabilized approach and manufacturer's recommended airspeed, or in its absence, not more than 1.3 V_{SO}, ±5 knots, with wind gust factor applied.
5. Makes smooth, timely, and correct control application during the round out and touchdown.
6. Touches down softly, with no drift, and with the airplane's longitudinal axis aligned with the runway/landing path.

7. Maintains crosswind correction and directional control throughout the approach and landing sequence.
8. Maintains proper position of the flight controls and sufficient speed to taxi on the soft surface.
9. Utilizes after landing runway incursion avoidance procedures.
10. Completes appropriate checklist.

Task E: Short-Field Takeoff (Confined Area—ASES) and Maximum Performance Climb (ASEL and ASES)

References: FAA-H-8083-3, FAA-H-8083-23; POH/AFM.

Objective: To determine that the applicant:

1. Utilizes procedures before taxiing onto the runway or takeoff area to ensure runway incursion avoidance. Verify ATC clearance/no aircraft on final at non-towered airports before entering the runway, and ensure that the aircraft is on the correct takeoff runway.
2. Exhibits satisfactory knowledge of the elements related to a short-field (confined area ASES) takeoff and maximum performance climb.
3. Positions the flight controls for the existing wind conditions, sets flaps as recommended.
4. Clears the area; taxies into takeoff position utilizing maximum available takeoff area and aligns the airplane on the runway center/takeoff path.
5. Selects an appropriate takeoff path for the existing conditions (ASES).
6. Applies brakes (if appropriate) while advancing the throttle smoothly to takeoff power.
7. Establishes and maintains the most efficient planing/lift off attitude and corrects for proposing and skipping (ASES).
8. Rotates and lifts off at the recommended airspeed, and accelerates to recommended obstacle clearance airspeed, or V_X.
9. Establishes a pitch attitude that will maintain the recommended obstacle clearance airspeed, or V_X,+5/-0 knots, until the obstacle is cleared, or until the airplane is 50 feet above the surface.
10. After clearing the obstacle, establishes the pitch attitude for V_Y, accelerates to V_Y, and maintains V_Y, ±5 knots, during the climb.
11. Retracts the landing gear, if appropriate, and flaps after clear of any obstacles or as recommended by manufacturer.

12. Maintains takeoff power and V_Y ±5 knots to a safe maneuvering altitude.
13. Maintains directional control and proper wind-drift correction throughout the takeoff and climb.
14. Completes appropriate checklist.

Task F: Short-Field Approach (Confined Area—ASES) and Landing (ASEL and ASES)

References: FAA-H-8083-3, FAA-H-8083-23; POH/AFM.

Objective: To determine that the applicant:

1. Exhibits satisfactory knowledge of the elements related to a short-field (confined area ASES) approach and landing.
2. Adequately surveys the intended landing area (ASES).
3. Considers the wind conditions, landing surface, obstructions, and selects the most suitable touchdown point.
4. Establishes the recommended approach and landing configuration and airspeed; adjusts pitch attitude and power.
5. Maintains a stabilized approach and recommended approach airspeed, or in its absence, not more than 1.3 V_{SO}, ±5 knots, with wind gust factor applied.
6. Makes smooth, timely, and correct control application during the round out and touchdown.
7. Selects the proper landing path, contacts the water at the minimum safe airspeed with the proper pitch attitude for the surface conditions (ASES).
8. Touches down smoothly at minimum control airspeed (ASEL).
9. Touches down within the available runway or water landing area, at or within 100 feet beyond a specified point, with no side drift, minimum float, and with the airplane's longitudinal axis aligned with and over the runway center/landing path.
10. Maintains crosswind correction and directional control throughout the approach and landing sequence.
11. Applies brakes (ASEL), or elevator control (ASES), as necessary, to stop in the shortest distance consistent with safety.
12. Utilizes after landing runway incursion avoidance procedures.
13. Completes appropriate checklist.

Task G: *Glassy Water Takeoff and Climb (ASES)*

NOTE: *If a glassy water condition does not exist, the applicant shall be evaluated by simulating the Task.*

References: FAA-H-8083-23; POH/AFM.

Objective: To determine that the applicant:

1. Exhibits knowledge of the elements related to glassy water takeoff and climb.
2. Positions the flight controls and flaps for the existing conditions.
3. Clears the area; selects an appropriate takeoff path considering surface hazards and/or vessels and surface conditions.
4. Retracts the water rudders as appropriate; advances the throttle smoothly to takeoff power.
5. Establishes and maintains an appropriate planing attitude, directional control, and corrects for porpoising, skipping, and increases in water drag.
6. Utilizes appropriate techniques to lift seaplane from the water considering surface conditions.
7. Establishes proper attitude/airspeed, and accelerates to V_Y, ±5 knots during the climb.
8. Retracts the landing gear, if appropriate, and flaps after a positive rate of climb is established.
9. Maintains takeoff power and V_Y ±5 knots to a safe maneuvering altitude.
10. Maintains directional control and proper wind-drift correction throughout takeoff and climb.
11. Completes the appropriate checklist.

Task H: *Glassy Water Approach and Landing (ASES)*

NOTE: *If a glassy water condition does not exist, the applicant shall be evaluated by simulating the Task.*

References: FAA-H-8083-23; POH/AFM.

Objective: To determine that the applicant:

1. Exhibits satisfactory knowledge of the elements related to glassy water approach and landing.
2. Adequately surveys the intended landing area.
3. Considers the wind conditions, water depth, hazards, surrounding terrain, and other watercraft.

4. Selects the most suitable approach path, and touchdown area.
5. Establishes the recommended approach and landing configuration and airspeed, and adjusts pitch attitude and power as required.
6. Maintains a stabilized approach and the recommended approach airspeed, ±5 knots and maintains a touchdown pitch attitude and descent rate from the last altitude reference until touchdown.
7. Makes smooth, timely, and correct power and control adjustments to maintain proper pitch attitude and rate of descent to touchdown; touching down in the first one-third of the water landing area.
8. Contacts the water in the proper pitch attitude, and slows to idle taxi speed.
9. Maintains crosswind correction and directional control throughout the approach and landing sequence.
10. Completes the appropriate checklist.

Task I: Rough Water Takeoff and Climb (ASES)

NOTE: If a rough water condition does not exist, the applicant shall be evaluated by simulating the Task.

References: FAA-H-8083-23; POH/AFM.

Objective: To determine that the applicant:

1. Exhibits satisfactory knowledge of the elements related to rough water takeoff and climb.
2. Positions the flight controls and flaps for the existing conditions.
3. Clears the area; selects an appropriate takeoff path considering wind, swells surface hazards and/or vessels.
4. Retracts the water rudders as appropriate; advances the throttle smoothly to takeoff power.
5. Establishes and maintains an appropriate planing attitude, directional control, and corrects for proposing, skipping, or excessive bouncing.
6. Rotates and lifts off at minimum airspeed and accelerates to V_Y, ±5 knots before leaving ground effect.
7. Retracts the landing gear, if appropriate, and flaps after a positive rate of climb is established.
8. Maintains takeoff power and V_Y ±5 knots to a safe maneuvering altitude.
9. Maintains directional control and proper wind-drift correction throughout takeoff and climb.
10. Completes the appropriate checklist.

Task J: Rough Water Approach and Landing (ASES)

NOTE: *If a rough water condition does not exist, the applicant shall be evaluated by simulating the Task.*

References: *FAA-H-8083-23; POH/AFM.*

Objective: To determine that the applicant:

1. Exhibits satisfactory knowledge of the elements related to rough water approach and landing.
2. Adequately surveys the intended landing area.
3. Considers the wind conditions, water, depth, hazards, surrounding terrain, and other watercraft.
4. Selects the most suitable approach path, and touchdown area.
5. Establishes the recommended approach and landing configuration and airspeed, and adjusts pitch attitude and power as required.
6. Maintains a stabilized approach and the recommended approach airspeed, or in its absence not more than 1.3 V_{SO} ±5 knots with wind gust factor applied.
7. Makes smooth, timely, and correct power and control application during the round out and touch down.
8. Contacts the water in the proper pitch attitude, and at the proper airspeed, considering the type of rough water.
9. Maintains crosswind correction and directional control throughout the approach and landing sequence.
10. Completes the appropriate checklist.

Task K: Power-Off 180° Accuracy Approach and Landing (ASEL and ASES)

Reference: *FAA-H-8083-3.*

Objective: To determine that the applicant:

1. Exhibits satisfactory knowledge of the elements related to a power-off 180° accuracy approach and landing.
2. Considers the wind conditions, landing surface, obstructions, and selects an appropriate touchdown point.
3. Positions airplane on downwind leg, parallel to landing runway, and not more than 1,000 feet AGL.
4. Completes final airplane configuration.
5. Touches down in a normal landing attitude, at or within 200 feet beyond the specified touchdown point.
6. Completes the appropriate checklist.

Task L: *Go-Around/Rejected Landing (ASEL and ASES)*

References: FAA-H-8083-3, FAA-H-8083-23; POH/AFM.

Objective: To determine that the applicant:

1. Exhibits satisfactory knowledge of the elements related to a go-around/rejected landing, with emphasis on factors that contribute to landing conditions that may require a go-around.
2. Makes a timely decision to discontinue the approach to landing.
3. Applies takeoff power immediately and transitions to climb pitch attitude for V_X or V_Y as appropriate +10/–5 knots and/or appropriate pitch attitude.
4. Retracts flaps as appropriate.
5. Retracts the landing gear if appropriate after a positive rate of climb is established.
6. Maneuvers to the side of runway/landing area to clear and avoid conflicting traffic.
7. Maintains takeoff power and V_Y ±5 knots to a safe maneuvering altitude.
8. Maintains directional control and proper wind-drift correction throughout the climb.
9. Completes the appropriate checklist.

V. Performance Maneuvers

NOTE: *The examiner shall at least select either Task A or B, and either C or D.*

Task A: Steep Turns (ASEL and ASES)

References: FAA-H-8083-3; POH/AFM.

Objective: To determine that the applicant:

1. Exhibits satisfactory knowledge of the elements related to steep turns.
2. Establishes the manufacturer's recommended airspeed or if one is not stated, a safe airspeed not to exceed V_A.
3. Rolls into a coordinated 360° steep turn with at least a 50° bank, followed by a 360° steep turn in the opposite direction.
4. Divides attention between airplane control and orientation.
5. Maintains the entry altitude, ±100 feet, airspeed, ±10 knots, bank, ±5°; and rolls out on the entry heading, ±10°.

Task B: Steep Spiral (ASEL and ASES)

Reference: FAA-H-8083-3.

Objective: To determine that the applicant:

1. Exhibits satisfactory knowledge of the elements related to a steep spiral, not to exceed 60° angle of bank to maintain a constant radius about a point.
2. Selects an altitude sufficient to continue through a series of at least three 360° turns.
3. Selects a suitable ground reference point.
4. Applies wind-drift correction to track a constant radius circle around selected reference point with bank not to exceed 60° at steepest point in turn.
5. Divides attention between airplane control and ground track, while maintaining coordinated flight.
6. Maintains the specified airspeed, ±10 knots, rolls out toward object or specified heading, ±10°.

Task C: Chandelles (ASEL and ASES)

Reference: FAA-H-8083-3.

Objective: To determine that the applicant:

1. Exhibits satisfactory knowledge of the elements related to chandelles.
2. Selects an altitude that will allow the maneuver to be performed no lower than 1,500 feet AGL.
3. Establishes the recommended entry configuration, power, and airspeed.
4. Establishes the angle of bank at approximately 30°.
5. Simultaneously applies power and pitch to maintain a smooth, coordinated climbing turn to the 90° point, with a constant bank.
6. Begins a coordinated constant rate rollout from the 90° point to the 180° point maintaining power and a constant pitch attitude.
7. Completes rollout at the 180° point, ±10° just above a stall airspeed, and maintaining that airspeed momentarily avoiding a stall.
8. Resumes straight-and-level flight with minimum loss of altitude.

Task D: Lazy Eights (ASEL and ASES)

Reference: *FAA-H-8083-3.*

Objective: To determine that the applicant:

1. Exhibits satisfactory knowledge of the elements related to lazy eights.
2. Selects an altitude that will allow the task to be performed no lower than 1,500 feet AGL.
3. Establishes the recommended entry configuration, power, and airspeed.
4. Maintains coordinated flight throughout the maneuver.
5. Achieves the following throughout the maneuver—

    a. approximately 30° bank at the steepest point.
    b. constant change of pitch and roll rate.
    c. altitude tolerance at 180° point, ±100 feet from entry altitude.
    d. airspeed tolerance at the 180° point, plus ±10 knots from entry airspeed.
    e. heading tolerance at the 180° point, ±10°.

6. Continues the maneuver through the number of symmetrical loops specified and resumes straight-and-level flight.

VI. Ground Reference Maneuver

Task A: Eights On Pylons (ASEL and ASES)

Reference: FAA-H-8083-3.

Objective: To determine that the applicant:

1. Exhibits satisfactory knowledge of the elements related to eights on pylons.
2. Determines the approximate pivotal altitude.
3. Selects suitable pylons that will permit straight-and-level flight between the pylons.
4. Enters the maneuver at the appropriate altitude and airspeed and at a bank angle of approximately 30° to 40° at the steepest point.
5. Applies the necessary corrections so that the line-of-sight reference line remains on the pylon.
6. Divides attention between accurate coordinated airplane control and outside visual references.
7. Holds pylon using appropriate pivotal altitude avoiding slips and skids.

VII. Navigation

Task A: Pilotage and Dead Reckoning (ASEL and ASES)

References: FAA-H-8083-25; Navigation Chart.

Objective: To determine that the applicant:

1. Exhibits satisfactory knowledge of the elements related to pilotage and dead reckoning.
2. Follows the preplanned course by reference to landmarks.
3. Identifies landmarks by relating surface features to chart symbols.
4. Navigates by means of precomputed headings, groundspeeds, and elapsed time.
5. Demonstrates the use of magnetic compass in navigation, to include turns to new headings.
6. Corrects for and records differences between preflight groundspeed and heading calculations and those determined en route.
7. Verifies the airplane's position within 2 nautical miles of flight planned route.
8. Arrives at the en route checkpoints within 3 minutes of the initial or revised ETA and provides a destination estimate.
9. Maintains appropriate altitude, ±100 feet, and headings, ±10°.

Task B: Navigation Systems and Radar Services (ASEL and ASES)

References: FAA-H-8083-3, FAA-H-8083-25; Navigation Equipment Operation Manuals; AIM; FAA-H-8083-2.

Objective: To determine that the applicant:

1. Exhibits satisfactory knowledge of the elements related to navigation systems and radar services.
2. Demonstrates the ability to use an airborne electronic navigation system.
3. Locates the airplane's position using the navigation system.
4. Intercepts and tracks a given course, radial, or bearing as appropriate.
5. Recognizes and describes the indication of station passage if appropriate.
6. Recognizes signal loss and takes appropriate action.
7. Uses proper communication procedures when utilizing radar services.

8. Maintains the appropriate altitude, ±100 feet and heading, ±10°.

Task C: Diversion (ASEL and ASES)

References: FAA-H-8083-25; AIM; Navigation Chart.

Objective: To determine that the applicant:

1. Exhibits satisfactory knowledge of the elements related to diversion.
2. Selects an appropriate alternate airport and route.
3. Makes an accurate estimate of heading, groundspeed, arrival time, and fuel consumption to the alternate airport.
4. Maintains the appropriate altitude, ±100 feet, and heading, ±10°.

Task D: Lost Procedures (ASEL and ASES)

References: FAA-H-8083-25; AIM; Navigation Chart.

Objective: To determine that the applicant:

1. Exhibits satisfactory knowledge of the elements related to lost procedures.
2. Selects an appropriate course of action.
3. Maintains an appropriate heading and climbs, if necessary.
4. Identifies prominent landmarks.
5. Uses navigation systems/facilities and/or contacts an ATC facility for assistance, as appropriate.

VIII. Slow Flight and Stalls

> *NOTE: In accordance with FAA policy, all stalls for the Commercial Certificate/Rating will be taken to the "onset" (buffeting) stall condition.*

Task A: Maneuvering During Slow Flight (ASEL and ASES)

References: FAA-H-8083-3; POH/AFM.

Objective: To determine that the applicant:

1. Exhibits satisfactory knowledge of the elements related to maneuvering during slow flight.
2. Selects an entry altitude that will allow the task to be completed no lower than 1,500 feet AGL.
3. Establishes and maintains an airspeed at which any further increase in angle of attack, increase in load factor, or reduction in power, would result in an immediate stall.
4. Accomplishes coordinated straight-and-level flight, turns, climbs, and descents with landing gear and flap configurations specified by the examiner.
5. Divides attention between airplane control and orientation.
6. Maintains the specified altitude, ±50 feet; specified heading, ±10°; airspeed +5/-0 knots, and specified angle of bank, ±5°.

Task B: Power-Off Stalls (ASEL and ASES)

References: FAA-H-8083-3; AC 61-67; POH/AFM.

> *NOTE: When published, the aircraft manufacturer's procedures for the specific make/mode/series aircraft take precedent over the identification and recovery procedures described in paragraphs 6, 7, and 8 below.*

Objective: To determine that the applicant:

1. Exhibits satisfactory knowledge of the elements related to power-off stalls.
2. Selects an entry altitude that allows the task to be completed no lower than 1,500 feet (460 meters) AGL.
3. Establishes a stabilized descent approximating a 3 degree final approach or landing descent rate in the landing configuration, as specified by the examiner.

4. Transitions smoothly from the approach or landing attitude to a pitch attitude that will induce a stall.
5. Maintains a specified heading, ±10°, if in straight flight; maintains a specified angle of bank, not to exceed 20°, ±5°, if in turning flight while inducing the stall.
6. Recognizes and recovers promptly at the "onset" (buffeting) stall condition.

NOTE: *Evaluation criteria for a recovery from an approach to stall should not mandate a predetermined value for altitude loss and should not mandate maintaining altitude during recovery. Proper evaluation criteria should consider the multitude of external and internal variables which affect the recovery altitude.*

7. Retracts the flaps to the recommended setting, retracts the landing gear if retractable after a positive rate of climb is established.
8. Accelerates to V_X or V_Y speed before the final flap retraction; returns to the normal climb attitude, airspeed, and configuration or an altitude, heading, and airspeed specified by the examiner.

Task C: *Power-On Stalls (ASEL and ASES)*

NOTE: *In some high performance airplanes, the power setting may have to be reduced below the practical test standards guideline power setting to prevent excessively high pitch attitudes (greater than 30° nose up).*

References: FAA-H-8083-3; POH/AFM.

Objective: To determine that the applicant:

1. Exhibits satisfactory knowledge of the elements related to power-on stalls.
2. Selects an entry altitude that allows the task to be completed no lower than 1,500 feet (460 meters) AGL.
3. Establishes the takeoff or departure configuration as specified by the examiner. Sets power to no less than 65 percent available power.
4. Transitions smoothly from the takeoff or departure attitude to a pitch attitude that will induce a stall.
5. Maintains a specified heading ±10°, in straight flight; maintains a specified angle of bank, not to exceed a 20°, ±10°, in turning flight, while inducing the stall.

6. Recognizes and recovers promptly at the "onset" (buffeting) stall condition.

NOTE: Evaluation criteria for a recovery from an approach to stall should not mandate a predetermined value for altitude loss and should not mandate maintaining altitude during recovery. Proper evaluation criteria should consider the multitude of external and internal variables which affect the recovery altitude.

7. Retracts flaps to the recommended setting, retracts the landing gear, if retractable, after a positive rate of climb is established.
8. Accelerates to V_X or V_Y speed before the final flap retraction; returns to the normal climb attitude, airspeed, and configuration or an altitude, heading, and airspeed specified by the examiner.

Task D: Accelerated Stalls (ASEL and ASES)

References: FAA-H-8083-3; AC 61-67; POH/AFM.

Objective: To determine that the applicant:

1. Exhibits satisfactory knowledge of the elements related to accelerated (power on or power off) stalls.
2. Selects an entry altitude that allows the task to be completed no lower than 3,000 feet AGL.
3. Establishes the airplane in a steady flight condition, airspeed below V_A, 20 knots above unaccelerated stall speed or the manufacturer's recommendations.
4. Transitions smoothly from the cruise attitude to the angle of bank of approximately 45° that will induce a stall.
5. Maintains coordinated turning flight, increasing elevator back pressure steadily and firmly to induce the stall.
6. Recognizes and recovers promptly at the "onset" (buffeting) stall condition.
7. Returns to the altitude, heading, and airspeed specified by the examiner.

Task E: Spin Awareness (ASEL and ASES)

References: FAA-H-8083-3; AC 61-67; POH/AFM.

Objective: To determine that the applicant exhibits satisfactory knowledge of the elements related to spin awareness by explaining:

1. Aerodynamic factors related to spins.
2. Flight situations where unintentional spins may occur.
3. Procedures for recovery from unintentional spins.

IX. Emergency Operations

Task A: Emergency Descent (ASEL and ASES)

References: FAA-H-8083-3; POH/AFM.

Objective: To determine that the applicant:

1. Exhibits satisfactory knowledge of the elements related to an emergency descent.
2. Recognizes situations, such as depressurization, cockpit smoke and/or fire that require an emergency descent.
3. Establishes the appropriate airspeed, ±10 knots, and configuration for the emergency descent.
4. Exhibits orientation, division of attention, and proper planning.
5. Maintains positive load factors during the descent.
6. Maintains appropriate airspeed, +0/−10 knots, and levels off at specified altitude, ±100 feet.
7. Completes appropriate checklists.

Task B: Emergency Approach and Landing (Simulated) (ASEL and ASES)

References: FAA-H-8083-3, FAA-H-8083-23; POH/AFM.

Objective: To determine that the applicant:

1. Exhibits satisfactory knowledge of the elements related to emergency approach and landing procedures.
2. Analyzes the situation and selects an appropriate course of action.
3. Establishes and maintains the recommended best glide airspeed, ±10 knots.
4. Selects a suitable landing area.
5. Plans and follows a flight pattern to the selected landing area considering altitude, wind, terrain, and obstructions.
6. Prepares for landing, or go-around, as specified by the examiner.
7. Follows the appropriate checklist.

Task C: Systems and Equipment Malfunctions (ASEL and ASES)

References: FAA-H-8083-3; POH/AFM.

Objective: To determine that the applicant:

1. Exhibits satisfactory knowledge of the elements related to systems and equipment malfunctions appropriate to the airplane provided for the practical test.
2. Analyzes the situation and takes appropriate action for simulated emergencies appropriate to the airplane provided for the practical test for at least three of the following:

   a. partial or complete power loss.
   b. engine roughness or overheat.
   c. carburetor or induction icing.
   d. loss of oil pressure.
   e. fuel starvation.
   f. electrical malfunction.
   g. vacuum/pressure, and associated flight instruments malfunction.
   h. pitot/static system malfunction.
   i. landing gear or flap malfunction.
   j. inoperative trim.
   k. inadvertent door or window opening.
   l. structural icing.
   m. smoke/fire/engine compartment fire.
   n. any other emergency appropriate to the airplane.

3. Follows the appropriate checklist or procedure.

Task D: Emergency Equipment and Survival Gear (ASEL and ASES)

References: FAA-H-8083-3; POH/AFM.

Objective: To determine that the applicant:

1. Exhibits satisfactory knowledge of the elements related to emergency equipment and survival gear appropriate to the airplane and environment encountered during flight. Identifies appropriate equipment that should be aboard the airplane.

X. High Altitude Operations

Task A: Supplemental Oxygen (ASEL and ASES)

References: 14 CFR part 91; FAA-H-8083-25; AC 61-107; AIM; POH/AFM.

Objective: To determine that the applicant exhibits satisfactory knowledge of the elements related to supplemental oxygen by explaining:

1. Supplemental oxygen requirements for flight crew and passengers when operating non-pressurized airplanes.
2. Identification and differences between "aviator's breathing oxygen" and other types of oxygen.
3. Operational characteristics of continuous flow, demand, and pressure-demand oxygen systems.

Task B: Pressurization (ASEL and ASES)

References: FAA-H-8083-3, FAA-H-8083-25A; AC 61-107; AIM; POH/AFM.

Objective: To determine that the applicant:

1. Exhibits satisfactory knowledge of the elements related to pressurization by explaining—

   a. fundamental concept of cabin pressurization.
   b. supplemental oxygen requirements when operating airplanes with pressurized cabins.
   c. physiological hazards associated with high altitude flight and decompression.

NOTE: Element 2 applies only if the airplane provided for the practical test is equipped for pressurized flight operations.

2. Operates the pressurization system properly, and reacts appropriately to simulated pressurization malfunctions.

XI. Postflight Procedures

Task A: After Landing, Parking, and Securing (ASEL and ASES)

NOTE: *The examiner shall select Task A and for ASES applicants at least one other Task.*

References: *FAA-H-8083-3, FAA-H-8083-23; POH/AFM.*

Objective: To determine that the applicant:

1. Exhibits satisfactory knowledge of the elements related to after landing, parking, and securing procedures.
2. Maintains directional control after touchdown while decelerating to an appropriate speed.
3. Observes runway hold lines and other surface control markings and lighting.
4. Parks in an appropriate area, considering the safety of nearby persons and property.
5. Follows the appropriate procedure for engine shutdown.
6. Completes the appropriate checklist.
7. Conducts an appropriate post flight inspection and secures the aircraft.

Task B: Anchoring (ASES)

References: *FAA-H-8083-23; POH/AFM.*

Objective: To determine that the applicant:

1. Exhibits satisfactory knowledge of the elements related to anchoring.
2. Selects a suitable area for anchoring, considering seaplane movement, water depth, tide, wind, and weather changes.
3. Uses an adequate number of anchors and lines of sufficient strength and length to ensure the seaplane's security.

Task C: Docking and Mooring (ASES)

References: *FAA-H-8083-23; POH/AFM.*

Objective: To determine that the applicant:

1. Exhibits satisfactory knowledge of the elements related to docking and mooring.

2. Approaches the dock or mooring buoy in the proper direction considering speed, hazards, wind, and water current.
3. Ensures seaplane security.

Task D: Ramping/Beaching (ASES)

References: FAA-H-8083-23; POH/AFM.

Objective: To determine that the applicant:

1. Exhibits satisfactory knowledge of the elements related to ramping/beaching.
2. Approaches the ramp/beach considering persons and property, in the proper attitude and direction, at a safe speed, considering water depth, tide, current and wind.
3. Ramps/beaches and secures the seaplane in a manner that will protect it from the harmful effect of wind, waves, and changes in water level.

(this page intentionally left blank)

Appendix 1

Task vs. Simulation Device Credit

Single-Engine Land (SEL)

(this page intentionally left blank)

Airplane Single-Engine Land

Task vs. Simulation Device Credit

Examiners conducting the Commercial Pilot–Airplane Practical Tests with flight simulation devices should consult appropriate documentation to ensure that the device has been approved for training, testing, or checking. The documentation for each device should reflect that the following activities have occurred:

1. The device must be evaluated, determined to meet the appropriate standards, and assigned the appropriate qualification level by the National Simulator Program Manager. The device must continue to meet qualification standards through continuing evaluations as outlined in the appropriate advisory circular (AC) or 14 CFR part 60. For airplane flight training devices (FTDs), AC 120-45 (as amended), Airplane Flight Training Device Qualifications, will be used. For simulators, AC 120-40 (as amended), Airplane Simulator Qualification or part 60 will be used.

2. The FAA must approve the device for training, testing, and checking the specific flight Tasks listed in this appendix.

3. The device must continue to support the level of student or applicant performance required by this PTS.

NOTE: *Users of the following chart are cautioned that use of the chart alone is incomplete. The description and objective of each Task as listed in the body of the PTS, including all notes, must also be incorporated for accurate simulation device use.*

Use of Chart

- **X** Creditable.
- **A** Creditable if appropriate systems are installed and operating.
- ***** Asterisk items require use of FTD or simulator visual reference.

NOTES:

1. Use of Level 1, 2 or Level 3 FTDs is not authorized for the practical test required by this PTS.
2. For practical tests, not more than 50 % of the maneuvers may be accomplished in an FTD or simulator UNLESS:

    a. each maneuver has been satisfactorily accomplished for an instructor, in the appropriate airplane, not less than three (3) times,

OR

    b. the applicant has logged not less than 500 hours of flight time as a pilot in airplanes.

3. Not all Areas of Operation (AOO) and Tasks required by this PTS are listed in the appendix. The remaining AOO and Tasks must be accomplished in an airplane.

(this page intentionally left blank)

Flight Simulation Device Level

Areas of Operation	Flight Simulation Device Level								
	4	5	6	7	A	B	C	D
II. Preflight Procedures								
A. Preflight Inspection (Cockpit Only)	A	A	X	X	X	X	X	X
B. Cockpit Management	A	A	X	X	X	X	X	X
C. Engine Starting	A	A	X	X	X	X	X	X
D. Taxiing	–	–	–	–	–	–	X	X
G. Before Takeoff Check	A	A	X	X	X	X	X	X
IV. Takeoffs, Landings, and Go-Arounds								
A. Normal and Crosswind Takeoff and Climb	–	–	–	–	–	–	X	X
B. Normal and Crosswind Approach and Landing	–	–	–	–	–	–	X	X
E. Short-Field Takeoff and Climb	–	–	–	–	X	X	X	X
F. Short-Field Approach and Landing	–	–	–	–	–	–	X	X
L. Go-Around*/Rejected Landing	–	–	X	X	X	X	X	X
V. Performance Maneuvers								
A. Steep Turns	–	–	X	X	X	X	X	X
VII. Navigation*								
B. Navigation Systems and Radar Services	–	A	X	X	X	X	X	X
C. Diversion	–	A	X	X	X	X	X	X
D. Lost Procedures	–	A	X	X	X	X	X	X

71

Single-Engine Land

(this page intentionally left blank)

Flight Simulation Device Level

Areas of Operation	Flight Simulation Device Level								
	4	5	6	7	A	B	C	D
VIII. Slow Flight and Stalls								
A. Maneuvering During Slow Flight	–	–	X	X	X	X	X	X
IX. Emergency Operations								
A. Emergency Descent	–	–	X	X	X	X	X	X
B. Emergency Approach and Landing	–	–	–	–	–	–	X	X
C. Systems and Equipment Malfunctions	A	A	X	X	X	X	X	X
X. High Altitude Operations								
B. Pressurization	A	A	X	X	X	X	X	X
XI. Postflight Procedures								
A. After Landing, Parking, and Securing	A	A	X	X	X	X	X	X

(this page intentionally left blank)

Section 2:

Commercial Pilot—Airplane

Multiengine Land

and

Multiengine Sea

(this page intentionally left blank)

Additional Rating Task Table:

Airplane Multiengine Land

Addition of an Airplane Multiengine Land Rating to an existing Commercial Pilot Certificate							
Required Tasks are indicated by either the Task letter(s) that apply(s) or an indication that all or none of the Tasks must be tested based on the notes in each Area of Operation.							
COMMERCIAL PILOT RATING(S) HELD							
AREAS OF OPER-ATION	ASEL	ASES	AMES	RH	RG	Glider	Balloon	Airship
I	F,G,H	F,G,H	F,G	F,G,H	F,G,H	F,G,H	F,G,H	F,G,H
II	ALL	ALL	D, F	ALL	ALL	ALL	ALL	ALL
III	NONE	C	C	B,C	NONE	B,C	B,C	B,C
IV	A,B,C,D	A,B,C,D	A,B,C,D	A,B,C,D,I	A,B,C,D,I	A,B,C,D,I	A,B,C,D,I	A,B,C,D,I
V	ALL	ALL	NONE	ALL	ALL	ALL	ALL	ALL
VI	NONE	NONE	NONE	NONE	NONE	ALL	ALL	NONE
VII	ALL	ALL	NONE	ALL	ALL	ALL	ALL	ALL
VIII	ALL	ALL	B,D,E	ALL	ALL	ALL	ALL	ALL
IX	NONE	NONE	NONE	ALL	ALL	ALL	ALL	ALL
X	ALL	ALL	NONE	ALL	ALL	ALL	ALL	ALL
XI	NONE	A	A	A	A	A	A	A

Additional Rating Task Table:

Airplane Multiengine Sea

Addition of an Airplane Multiengine Sea Rating to an existing Commercial Pilot Certificate

Required Tasks are indicated by either the Task letter(s) that apply(s) or an indication that all or none of the Tasks must be tested based on the notes in each Area of Operation.

COMMERCIAL PILOT RATING(S) HELD

AREAS OF OPER-ATION	AMEL	ASEL	ASES	RH	RG	Glider	Balloon	Airship
I	F,G,I,J	F,G,H, I,J	F,G,H	F,G,H, I,J	F,G,H, I,J	F,G,H, I,J	F,G,H, I,J	F,G,H, I,J
II	E, F	ALL	ALL	ALL	ALL	ALL	ALL	ALL
III	C	C	NONE	B,C	C	B,C	B,C	B,C
IV	A,B,C, D,E,F, G,H	A,B,C, D,E,F, G,H	A,B,C, D,E,F, G,H	ALL	ALL	ALL	ALL	ALL
V	NONE	ALL	ALL	ALL	ALL	ALL	ALL	ALL
VI	NONE	NONE	NONE	NONE	NONE	ALL	ALL	NONE
VII	NONE	ALL	ALL	ALL	ALL	ALL	ALL	ALL
VIII	B,D,E	ALL	ALL	ALL	ALL	ALL	ALL	ALL
IX	NONE	NONE	NONE	ALL	ALL	ALL	ALL	ALL
X	NONE	ALL	ALL	ALL	ALL	ALL	ALL	ALL
XI	B,C,D	B,C,D	NONE	ALL	B,C,D	ALL	ALL	ALL

Applicant's Practical Test Checklist

Appointment with Examiner

Examiner's Name: _____

Location: _____

Date/TIme: _____

ACCEPTABLE AIRCRAFT
- ☐ Aircraft Documents:
  - ☐ Airworthiness Certificate
  - ☐ Registration Certificate
  - ☐ Operating Limitations
- ☐ Aircraft Maintenance Records:
  - ☐ Logbook Record of Airworthiness Inspections and AD Compliance
- ☐ Pilot's Operating Handbook, FAA-Approved Airplane Flight Manual

PERSONAL EQUIPMENT
- ☐ View-Limiting Device
- ☐ Current Aeronautical Charts
- ☐ Computer and Plotter
- ☐ Flight Plan Form
- ☐ Flight Logs
- ☐ Current AIM, Airport Facility Directory, and Appropriate Publications

PERSONAL RECORDS
- ☐ Identification—Photo/Signature ID
- ☐ Pilot Certificate
- ☐ Current and Appropriate Medical Certificate
- ☐ Completed FAA Form 8710-1, Airman Certificate and/or Rating Application with Instructor's Signature (If applicable)
- ☐ Computer Test Report
- ☐ Pilot Logbook with appropriate Instructor Endorsements
- ☐ FAA Form 8060-5, Notice of Disapproval (if applicable)
- ☐ Approved School Graduation Certificate (if applicable)
- ☐ Examiner's Fee (if applicable)

(this page intentionally left blank)

Examiner's Practical Test Checklist

Airplane Multiengine Land
and
Airplane Multiengine Sea

Applicant's Name: _____

Location: _____

Date/Time: _____

I. PREFLIGHT PREPARATION

- ☐ **A.** Certificates and Documents (AMEL and AMES)
- ☐ **B.** Airworthiness Requirements (AMEL and AMES)
- ☐ **C.** Weather Information (AMEL and AMES)
- ☐ **D.** Cross-Country Flight Planning (AMEL and AMES)
- ☐ **E.** National Airspace System (AMEL and AMES)
- ☐ **F.** Performance and Limitations (AMEL and AMES)
- ☐ **G.** Operation of Systems (AMEL and AMES)
- ☐ **H.** Principles of Flight—Engine Inoperative (AMEL and AMES)
- ☐ **I.** Water and Seaplane Characteristics (AMES)
- ☐ **J.** Seaplane Bases, Maritime Rules, and Aids to Marine Navigation (AMES)
- ☐ **K.** Aeromedical Factors (AMEL and AMES)

II. PREFLIGHT PROCEDURES

- ☐ **A.** Preflight Inspection (AMEL and AMES)
- ☐ **B.** Cockpit Management (AMEL and AMES)
- ☐ **C.** Engine Starting (AMEL and AMES)
- ☐ **D.** Taxiing (AMEL)
- ☐ **E.** Taxiing and Sailing (AMES)
- ☐ **F.** Runway Incursion Avoidance (AMEL and AMES)
- ☐ **G.** Before Takeoff Check (AMEL and AMES)

III. AIRPORT AND SEAPLANE BASE OPERATIONS

- ☐ **A.** Radio Communications and ATC Light Signals (AMEL and AMES)
- ☐ **B.** Traffic Patterns (AMEL and AMES)

☐   **C.** Airport/Seaplane Base, Runway, and Taxiway Signs, Markings, and Lighting (AMEL and AMES)

IV. TAKEOFFS, LANDINGS, AND GO-AROUNDS

☐   **A.** Normal and Crosswind Takeoff and Climb (AMEL and AMES)

☐   **B.** Normal and Crosswind Approach and Landing (AMEL and AMES)

☐   **C.** Short-Field Takeoff (Confined Area—AMEL) and Maximum Performance Climb (AMEL and AMES)

☐   **D.** Short-Field (Confined Area—AMES) Approach and Landing (AMEL and AMES)

☐   **E.** Glassy Water Takeoff and Climb (AMES)

☐   **F.** Glassy Water Approach and Landing (AMES)

☐   **G.** Rough Water Takeoff and Climb (AMES)

☐   **H.** Rough Water Approach and Landing (AMES)

☐   **I.** Go-Around/Rejected Landing (AMEL and AMES)

V. PERFORMANCE MANEUVER

☐   **A.** Steep Turns (AMEL and AMES)

VI. NAVIGATION

☐   **A.** Pilotage and Dead Reckoning (AMEL and AMES)

☐   **B.** Navigation Systems and Radar Services (AMEL and AMES)

☐   **C.** Diversion (AMEL and AMES)

☐   **D.** Lost Procedures (AMEL and AMES)

VII. SLOW FLIGHT AND STALLS

☐   **A.** Maneuvering During Slow Flight (AMEL and AMES)

☐   **B.** Power-Off Stalls (AMEL and AMES)

☐   **C.** Power-On Stalls (AMEL and AMES)

☐   **D.** Accelerated Stalls (AMEL and AMES)

☐   **E.** Spin Awareness (AMEL and AMES)

VIII. EMERGENCY OPERATIONS

☐   **A.** Emergency Descent (AMEL and AMES)

☐   **B.** Engine Failure During Takeoff Before V_{MC} (Simulated) (AMEL and AMES)

☐   **C.** Engine Failure After Lift-Off (Simulated) (AMEL and AMES)

☐ **D.** Approach and Landing with an Inoperative Engine (Simulated) (AMEL and AMES)

☐ **E.** Systems and Equipment Malfunctions (AMEL and AMES)

☐ **F.** Emergency Equipment and Survival Gear (AMEL and AMES)

IX. HIGH ALTITUDE OPERATIONS

☐ **A.** Supplemental Oxygen (AMEL and AMES)

☐ **B.** Pressurization (AMEL and AMES)

X. MULTIENGINE OPERATIONS

☐ **A.** Maneuvering with One Engine Inoperative (AMEL and AMES)

☐ **B.** V_{MC} Demonstration (AMEL and AMES)

☐ **C.** Engine Failure During Flight (by Reference to Instruments) (AMEL and AMES)

☐ **D.** Instrument Approach—One Engine Inoperative (by Reference to Instruments) (AMEL and AMES)

XI. POSTFLIGHT PROCEDURES

☐ **A.** After Landing, Parking, and Securing (AMEL and AMES)

☐ **B.** Anchoring (AMES)

☐ **C.** Docking and Mooring (AMES)

☐ **D.** Ramping/Beaching (AMES)

(this page intentionally left blank)

(Change 1 – March 13, 2012: Judgment Assessment Matrix removed)

(this page intentionally left blank)

Areas of Operation:

I. Preflight Preparation

NOTE: The examiner shall develop a scenario based on real time weather to evaluate Tasks C and D.

Task A: Certificates and Documents (AMEL and AMES)

References: 14 CFR parts 39, 43, 61, 91; FAA-H-8083-3, FAA-H-8083-25; POH/AFM.

Objective: To determine that the applicant exhibits satisfactory knowledge of the elements related to certificates and documents by:

1. Explaining—

   a. commercial pilot certificate privileges, limitations, and recent flight experience requirements.
   b. medical certificate class and duration.
   c. pilot logbook or flight records.

2. Locating and explaining—

   a. airworthiness and registration certificates.
   b. operating limitations, placards, instrument markings, and POH/AFM.
   c. weight and balance data and equipment list.

Task B: Airworthiness Requirements (AMEL and AMES)

References: 14 CFR parts 39, 91; FAA-H-8083-25.

Objective: To determine that the applicant exhibits satisfactory knowledge of the elements related to airworthiness requirements by:

1. Explaining—

   a. required instruments and equipment for day/night VFR.
   b. procedures and limitations for determining airworthiness of the airplane with inoperative instruments and equipment with and without an MEL.

c. requirements and procedures for obtaining a special flight permit.

2. Locating and explaining—

   a. airworthiness directives.
   b. compliance records.
   c. maintenance/inspection requirements.
   d. appropriate record keeping.

Task C: Weather Information (AMEL and AMES)

References: 14 CFR part 91; AC 00-6, AC 00-45, AC 61-84; FAA-H-8083-25; AIM.

Objective: To determine that the applicant:

1. Exhibits satisfactory knowledge of the elements related to weather information by analyzing weather reports, charts, and forecasts from various sources with emphasis on—

   a. METAR, TAF, and FA.
   b. surface analysis chart.
   c. radar summary chart.
   d. winds and temperature aloft chart.
   e. significant weather prognostic charts.
   f. convective outlook chart.
   g. AWOS, ASOS, and ATIS reports.
   h. SIGMETs and AIRMETs.
   i. PIREPs.
   j. windshear reports.
   k. icing and freezing level information.

2. Makes a competent "go/no-go" decision based on available weather information.

Task D: Cross-Country Flight Planning (AMEL and AMES)

References: 14 CFR part 91; FAA-H-8083-25; AC 61-84; Navigation Charts; AFD; AIM; NOTAMS.

Objective: To determine that the applicant:

1. Exhibits satisfactory knowledge of the elements related to cross-country flight planning by presenting and explaining a pre-planned VFR cross-country flight, as previously assigned by the examiner. On the day of the practical test,

the final flight plan shall be to the first fuel stop, based on maximum allowable passengers, baggage, and/or cargo loads using real-time weather.
2. Uses appropriate and current aeronautical charts.
3. Properly identifies airspace, obstructions, and terrain features.
4. Selects easily identifiable en route checkpoints.
5. Selects most favorable altitudes considering weather conditions and equipment capabilities.
6. Computes headings, flight time, and fuel requirements.
7. Selects appropriate navigation system/facilities and communication frequencies.
8. Applies pertinent information from AFD, NOTAMs, and NOTAMS relative to airport, runway and taxiway closures, and other flight publications.
9. Completes a navigation log and simulates filing a VFR flight plan.

Task E: National Airspace System (AMEL and AMES)

References: 14 CFR parts 71, 91, 93; Navigation Charts; AIM.

Objective: To determine that the applicant exhibits satisfactory knowledge of the elements related to the National Airspace System by explaining:

1. Basic VFR weather minimums—for all classes of airspace.
2. Airspace classes—their operating rules, pilot certification, and airplane equipment requirements for the following—

   a. Class A.
   b. Class B.
   c. Class C.
   d. Class D.
   e. Class E.
   f. Class G.

3. Special use, special flight rules areas, and other airspace areas.

Task F: Performance and Limitations (AMEL and AMES)

References: FAA-H-8083-1, FAA-H-8083-25; AC 61-84; POH/AFM.

Objective: To determine that the applicant:

1. Exhibits satisfactory knowledge of the elements related to performance and limitations by explaining the use of charts, tables, and data to determine performance and the adverse effects of exceeding limitations.
2. Computes weight and balance. Determines the computed weight and center of gravity are within the airplane's operating limitations and if the weight and center of gravity will remain within limits during all phases of flight.
3. Demonstrates use of the appropriate manufacturer's performance charts, tables, and data.
4. Describes the effects of atmospheric conditions on the airplane's performance.

Task G: Operation of Systems (AMEL and AMES)

References: FAA-H-8083-25; FAA-H-8083-23; POH/AFM.

Objective: To determine that the applicant exhibits satisfactory knowledge of the elements related to the operation of systems on the airplane provided for the flight test by explaining at least three of the following systems.

1. Primary flight controls and trim.
2. Flaps, leading edge devices, and spoilers.
3. Water rudders (ASES).
4. Powerplant and propeller.
5. Landing gear.
6. Fuel, oil, and hydraulic.
7. Electrical.
8. Avionics.
9. Pitot-static, vacuum/pressure, and associated flight instruments.
10. Environmental.
11. Deicing and anti-icing.

Task H: Principles of Flight—Engine Inoperative (AMEL and AMES)

References: FAA-H-8083-3, FAA-H-8083-25, FAA-P-8740-19; POH/AFM.

Objective: To determine that the applicant exhibits satisfactory knowledge of the elements related to engine inoperative principles of flight by explaining the:

1. meaning of the term "critical engine."
2. effects of density altitude on the V_{MC} demonstration.

3. effects of airplane weight and center of gravity on control.
4. effects of angle of bank on V_{MC}.
5. relationship of V_{MC} to stall speed.
6. reasons for loss of directional control.
7. indications of loss of directional control.
8. importance of maintaining the proper pitch and bank attitude, and the proper coordination of controls.
9. loss of directional control recovery procedure.
10. engine failure during takeoff including planning, decisions, and single-engine operations.

Task I: Water and Seaplane Characteristics (AMES)

Reference: FAA-H-8083-23.

Objective: To determine that the applicant exhibits satisfactory knowledge of the elements related to water and seaplane characteristics by explaining:

1. The characteristics of a water surface as affected by features, such as—

   a. size and location.
   b. protected and unprotected areas.
   c. surface wind.
   d. direction and strength of water current.
   e. floating and partially submerged debris.
   f. sandbars, islands, and shoals.
   g. vessel traffic and wakes.
   h. other features peculiar to the area.

2. Float and hull construction, and their effect on seaplane performance.
3. Causes of proposing and skipping, and the pilot action required to prevent or correct these occurrences.

Task J: Seaplane Bases, Maritime Rules, and Aids to Marine Navigation (AMES)

References: FAA-H-8083-3; AIM; USCG NAVIGATION Rules; International–Inland; POH/AFM; AFD.

Objective: To determine that the applicant exhibits satisfactory knowledge of the elements related to seaplane bases, maritime rules, and aids to marine navigation by explaining:

1. How to locate and identify seaplane bases on charts or in directories.
2. Operating restrictions at various bases.
3. Right-of-way, steering, and sailing rules pertinent to seaplane operation.
4. Marine navigation aids, such as buoys, beacons, lights, and sound signals.

Task K: Aeromedical Factors (AMEL and AMES)

References: FAA-H-8083-25; AIM.

Objective: To determine that the applicant exhibits satisfactory knowledge of the elements related to aeromedical factors by explaining:

1. The symptoms, causes, effects, and corrective actions of at least 4 of the following—

   a. hypoxia.
   b. hyperventilation.
   c. middle ear and sinus problems.
   d. spatial disorientation.
   e. motion sickness.
   f. carbon monoxide poisoning.
   g. stress and fatigue.
   h. dehydration.

2. The effects of alcohol, drugs, and over-the-counter medications.
3. The effects of excess nitrogen during scuba dives upon a pilot or passenger in flight.

II. Preflight Procedures

Task A: Preflight Inspection (AMEL and AMES)

References: FAA-H-8083-3, FAA-H-8083-23; POH/AFM.

Objective: To determine that the applicant:

1. Exhibits satisfactory knowledge of the elements related to preflight inspection. This shall include which items must be inspected, the reasons for checking each item, and how to detect possible defects.
2. Inspects the airplane with reference to an appropriate checklist.
3. Verifies the airplane is in condition for safe flight.

Task B: Cockpit Management (AMEL and AMES)

References: FAA-H-8083-3; POH/AFM.

Objective: To determine that the applicant:

1. Exhibits satisfactory knowledge of the elements related to cockpit management procedures.
2. Ensures all loose items in the cockpit and cabin are secured.
3. Organizes material and equipment in an efficient manner so they are readily available.
4. Briefs occupants on the use of safety belts, shoulder harnesses, doors, and emergency procedures.

Task C: Engine Starting (AMEL and AMES)

References: FAA-H-8083-3, FAA-H-8083-23, FAA-H-8083-25; AC 91-13; AC 91 55; POH/AFM.

Objective: To determine that the applicant:

1. Exhibits knowledge of the elements related to recommended engine starting procedures. This shall include the use of an external power source, and starting under various atmospheric conditions.
2. Positions the airplane properly considering structures, surface conditions, other aircraft, and the safety of nearby persons and property.
3. Utilizes the appropriate checklist for starting procedure.

Task D: Taxiing (AMEL)

References: FAA-H-8083-3; POH/AFM.

Objective: To determine that the applicant:

1. Exhibits satisfactory knowledge of the elements related to safe taxi procedures at towered and non-towered airports.
2. Performs a brake check immediately after the airplane begins moving.
3. Positions the flight controls properly for the existing wind conditions.
4. Controls direction and speed without excessive use of brakes.
5. Exhibits procedures for steering, maneuvering, maintaining taxiway, runway position, and situational awareness to avoid runway incursions.
6. Exhibits proper positioning of the aircraft relative to hold lines.
7. Exhibits procedures to insure clearances/instructions are received and recorded/read back correctly.
8. Exhibits situational awareness/taxi procedures in the event the aircraft is on a taxiway that is between parallel runways.
9. Uses a taxi chart during taxi.
10. Complies with airport/taxiway markings, signals, ATC clearances, and instructions.
11. Utilizes procedures for eliminating pilot distractions.
12. Taxiing to avoid other aircraft/vehicles and hazards.

Task E: Taxiing and Sailing (AMES)

References: FAA-H-8083-23; USCG Navigation Rules; International–Inland; POH/AFM.

Objective: To determine that the applicant:

1. Exhibits satisfactory knowledge of the elements related to water taxi and sailing procedures.
2. Positions the flight controls properly for the existing wind conditions.
3. Plans and follows the most favorable course while taxi or sailing. Considers wind, water current, water conditions, and maritime regulations.
4. Uses the appropriate idle, plow, or step taxi technique.
5. Uses flight controls, flaps, doors, water rudder, and power correctly so as to follow the desired course while sailing.
6. Prevents and corrects for proposing and skipping.
7. Avoids other aircraft, vessels, and hazards.

8. Complies with seaplane base signs, signals, and clearances.

Task F: **Runway Incursion Avoidance (AMEL and AMES)**

References: FAA-H-8083-3, FAA-H-8083-25; AC 91-73, AC 150-5340-18; AIM.

Objective: To determine that the applicant exhibits knowledge of the elements of runway incursion avoidance by:

1. Exhibiting distinct challenges and requirements during taxi operations not found in other phases of flight operations.
2. Exhibiting procedures for appropriate cockpit activities during taxiing including taxi route planning, briefing the location of HOT SPOTS, communicating and coordinating with ATC.
3. Exhibiting procedures for steering, maneuvering, maintaining taxiway, runway position, and situational awareness.
4. Knowing the relevance/importance of hold lines.
5. Exhibiting procedures to ensure the pilot maintains strict focus to the movement of the aircraft and ATC communications, including the elimination of all distractive activities (i.e. cell phone, texting, conversations with passengers) during aircraft taxi, takeoff and climb out to cruise altitude.
6. Utilizing procedures for holding the pilot's workload to a minimum during taxi operations.
7. Utilizing taxi operation planning procedures, such as recording taxi instructions, reading back taxi clearances, and reviewing taxi routes on the airport diagram.
8. Utilizing procedures to insure that clearance or instructions that are actually received are adhered to rather than the ones expected to be received.
9. Utilizing procedures to maintain/enhance situational awareness when conducting taxi operations in relation to other aircraft operations in the vicinity as well as to other vehicles moving on the airport.
10. Exhibiting procedures for briefing if a landing rollout to a taxiway exit will place the pilot in close proximity to another runway which can result in a runway incursion.
11. Conducting appropriate after landing/taxi procedures in the event the aircraft is on a taxiway that is between parallel runways.
12. Knowing specific procedures for operations at an airport with an operating air traffic control tower, with emphasis on

ATC communications and runway entry/crossing authorizations.
13. Utilizing ATC communications and pilot actions before takeoff, before landing, and after landing at towered and non-towered airports.
14. Knowing procedures unique to night operations.
15. Knowing operations at non-towered airports.
16. Knowing the use of aircraft exterior lighting.
17. Knowing the hazards of Low visibility operations.

Task G: Before Takeoff Check (AMEL and AMES)

References: FAA-H-8083-3, FAA-H-8083-23; POH/AFM.

Objective: To determine that the applicant:

1. Exhibits satisfactory knowledge of the elements related to the before takeoff check. This shall include the reasons for checking each item and how to detect malfunctions.
2. Positions the airplane properly considering other aircraft/vessels, wind and surface conditions.
3. Divides attention inside and outside the cockpit.
4. Ensures that engine temperatures and pressure are suitable for run-up and takeoff.
5. Accomplishes the before takeoff checklist and ensures the airplane is in safe operating condition as recommended by the manufacturer.
6. Reviews takeoff performance, such as airspeeds, takeoff distances, departure, and emergency procedures.
7. Avoids runway incursions and ensures no conflict with traffic prior to taxiing into takeoff position.

III. Airport and Seaplane Base Operations

Task A: Radio Communications and ATC Light Signals (AMEL and AMES)

References: 14 CFR part 91; FAA-H-8083-25; AIM.

Objective: To determine that the applicant:

1. Exhibits satisfactory knowledge of the elements related to radio communications and ATC light signals.
2. Selects appropriate frequencies.
3. Transmits using AIM specified phraseology and procedures.
4. Acknowledges radio communications and complies with instructions.

Task B: Traffic Patterns (AMEL and AMES)

References: FAA-H-8083-3, FAA-H-8083-25; AC 90-66; AIM.

Objective: To determine that the applicant:

1. Exhibits satisfactory knowledge of the elements related to traffic patterns. This shall include procedures at airports with and without operating control towers, prevention of runway incursions, collision avoidance, wake turbulence avoidance, and wind shear.
2. Complies with proper traffic pattern procedures.
3. Maintains proper spacing from other aircraft.
4. Corrects for wind drift to maintain the proper ground track.
5. Maintains orientation with the runway/landing area in use.
6. Maintains traffic pattern altitude, ±100 feet, and the appropriate airspeed, ±10 knots.

Task C: Airport/Seaplane Base, Runway, and Taxiway Signs, Markings, and Lighting (AMEL and AMES)

References: FAA-H-8083-23, FAA-H-8083-25; AIM; AFD; AC 91-73, AC 150-5340-18.

Objective: To determine that the applicant:

1. Exhibits satisfactory knowledge of the elements related to airport/seaplane base, runway, and taxiway operations with emphasis on runway incursion avoidance.

2. Properly identifies and interprets airport/seaplane base, runway, and taxiway signs, markings, and lighting, with emphasis on runway incursion avoidance.

IV. Takeoffs, Landings, and Go-Arounds

Task A: *Normal and Crosswind Takeoff and Climb (AMEL and AMES)*

NOTE: If a crosswind condition does not exist, the applicant's knowledge of crosswind elements shall be evaluated through oral testing.

References: FAA-H-8083-3, FAA-H-8083-23, FAA-P-8740-19; POH/AFM.

Objective: To determine that the applicant:

1. Utilizes procedures before taxiing onto the runway or takeoff area to ensure runway incursion avoidance. Verify ATC clearance/no aircraft on final at non-towered airports before entering the runway, and ensure that the aircraft is on the correct takeoff runway.
2. Exhibits satisfactory knowledge of the elements related to a normal and crosswind takeoff, climb operations, and rejected takeoff procedures.
3. Ascertains wind direction with or without visible wind direction indicators.
4. Calculates/determines if crosswind component is above his or her ability or that of the aircraft's capability.
5. Positions the flight controls for the existing wind conditions.
6. Clears the area, taxies onto the takeoff surface, and aligns the airplane on the runway center/takeoff path.
7. Retracts the water rudders as appropriate (AMES), and advances the throttle smoothly to takeoff power.
8. Establishes and maintains the most efficient planing/lift off attitude and corrects for proposing and skipping (AMES).
9. Rotates and lifts off at the recommended airspeed and accelerates to V_Y.
10. Establishes a pitch attitude that will maintain V_Y,±5 knots.
11. Retracts the landing gear if appropriate, and flaps after a positive rate of climb is established.
12. Maintains takeoff power and V_Y ±5 knots to a safe maneuvering altitude.
13. Maintains directional control, proper wind-drift correction throughout the takeoff and climb.
14. Complies with responsible environmental practices, including noise abatement procedures.
15. Completes appropriate checklists.

Task B: *Normal and Crosswind Approach and Landing (AMEL and AMES)*

NOTE: *If a crosswind condition does not exist, the applicant's knowledge of crosswind elements shall be evaluated through oral testing.*

References: *FAA-H-8083-3, FAA-H-8083-23; POH/AFM.*

Objective: To determine that the applicant:

1. Exhibits satisfactory knowledge of the elements related to a normal and crosswind approach and landing with emphasis on proper use and coordination of flight controls.
2. Adequately surveys the intended landing area (AMES).
3. Considers the wind conditions, landing surface, obstructions, and selects a suitable touchdown point.
4. Establishes the recommended approach and landing configuration and airspeed, and adjusts pitch attitude and power as required.
5. Maintains a stabilized approach and recommended airspeed established by the manufacturer, or in its absence, not more than 1.3 V_{SO}, +10/-5 knots, with wind gust factor applied.
6. Makes smooth, timely, and correct control application during the round out and touchdown.
7. Contacts the water at the proper pitch attitude (AMES).
8. Touches down smoothly at approximate stalling speed (AMEL).
9. Touches down within the first one-third of the available runway or water landing area, within 200 feet beyond a specified point, with no drift, and with the airplane's longitudinal axis aligned with and over the runway center/landing path.
10. Maintains crosswind correction and directional control throughout the approach and landing sequence.
11. Executes a timely go-around decision when the approach cannot be made within the tolerances listed above.
12. Utilizes after landing runway incursion avoidance procedures.
13. Completes the appropriate checklist.

Task C: *Short-Field Takeoff (Confined Area—AMEL) and Maximum Performance Climb (AMEL and AMES)*

References: *FAA-H-8083-3, FAA-H-8083-23, FAA-P-8740-19; POH/AFM.*

Objective: To determine that the applicant:

1. Utilizes procedures before taxiing onto the runway or takeoff area to ensure runway incursion avoidance. Verify ATC clearance/no aircraft on final at non-towered airports before entering the runway, and ensure that the aircraft is on the correct takeoff runway.
2. Exhibits satisfactory knowledge of the elements related to a short-field confined area (AMES) takeoff and maximum performance climb.
3. Positions the flight controls for the existing wind conditions, sets flaps as recommended.
4. Clears the area, taxies into takeoff position utilizing maximum available takeoff area, and aligns the airplane on the runway center/takeoff path.
5. Selects an appropriate take-off path for the existing conditions (AMES).
6. Applies brakes, if appropriate, while advancing the throttles smoothly to takeoff power.
7. Establishes and maintains the most efficient planing/lift off attitude and corrects for proposing and skipping (AMES).
8. Rotates and lifts off at the recommended airspeed, and accelerates to recommended obstacle clearance airspeed, or V_X.
9. Establishes a pitch attitude that will maintain the recommended obstacle clearance airspeed, or V_X, +5/-0 knots, until the obstacle is cleared, or until the airplane is 50 feet above the surface.
10. After clearing the obstacle, establishes the pitch attitude for V_Y, accelerates to V_Y, and maintains V_Y, ±5 knots, during the climb.
11. Retracts the landing gear, if appropriate, and flaps after clear of any obstacles or as recommended by manufacturer.
12. Maintains takeoff power and V_Y ±5 knots to a safe maneuvering altitude.
13. Maintains directional control and proper wind-drift correction throughout the takeoff and climb.
14. Completes appropriate checklist.

Task D: Short-Field (Confined Area—AMES) Approach and Landing (AMEL and AMES)

References: FAA-H-8083-3, FAA-H-8083-23; POH/AFM.

Objective: To determine that the applicant:

1. Exhibits satisfactory knowledge of the elements related to a short-field (confined area AMES) approach and landing.
2. Adequately surveys the intended landing area (AMES).
3. Considers the wind conditions, landing surface, obstructions, and selects the most suitable touchdown point.
4. Establishes the recommended approach and landing configuration and airspeed; adjusts pitch attitude and power as required.
5. Maintains a stabilized approach and recommended approach airspeed, or in its absence, not more than 1.3 V_{SO}, ±5 knots, with wind gust factor applied.
6. Makes smooth, timely, and correct control application during the round out and touchdown.
7. Selects the proper landing path, contacts the water at the minimum safe airspeed with the proper pitch attitude for the surface conditions (AMES).
8. Touches down smoothly at minimum control airspeed (AMEL).
9. Touches down at or within 100 feet beyond a specified point, with no side drift, minimum float, and with the airplane's longitudinal axis aligned with and over the runway center/landing path.
10. Maintains crosswind correction and directional control throughout the approach and landing sequence.
11. Applies brakes (AMEL) or elevator control (AMES), as necessary, to stop in the shortest distance consistent with safety.
12. Utilizes after landing runway incursion avoidance procedures.
13. Completes appropriate checklist.

Task E: Glassy Water Takeoff and Climb (AMES)

NOTE: If a glassy water condition does not exist, the applicant shall be evaluated by simulating the Task.

References: FAA-H-8083-23, FAA-P-8740-19; POH/AFM.

Objective: To determine that the applicant:

1. Exhibits knowledge of the elements related to glassy water takeoff and climb.
2. Positions the flight controls and flaps for the existing conditions.
3. Clears the area; selects an appropriate takeoff path considering surface hazards and/or vessels and surface conditions.

4. Retracts the water rudders as appropriate; advances the throttle smoothly to takeoff power.
5. Establishes and maintains an appropriate planing attitude, directional control, and corrects for proposing, skipping, and increases in water drag.
6. Utilizes appropriate techniques to lift seaplane from the water considering surface conditions.
7. Establishes proper attitude/airspeed, and accelerates to V_Y, ±5 knots during the climb.
8. Retracts the landing gear, if appropriate, and flaps after a positive rate of climb is established.
9. Maintains takeoff power and V_Y ±5 knots to a safe maneuvering altitude.
10. Maintains directional control and proper wind-drift correction throughout takeoff and climb.
11. Completes the appropriate checklist.

Task F: Glassy Water Approach and Landing (AMES)

NOTE: *If a glassy water condition does not exist, the applicant shall be evaluated by simulating the Task.*

References: FAA-H-8083-23; POH/AFM.

Objective: To determine that the applicant:

1. Exhibits satisfactory knowledge of the elements related to glassy water approach and landing.
2. Adequately surveys the intended landing area.
3. Considers the wind conditions, water depth, hazards, surrounding terrain, and other watercraft.
4. Selects the most suitable approach path and touchdown area.
5. Establishes the recommended approach and landing configuration and airspeed, and adjusts pitch attitude and power as required.
6. Maintains a stabilized approach and the recommended approach airspeed, ±5 knots, and maintains a touchdown pitch attitude and descent rate from the last altitude reference until touchdown.
7. Makes smooth, timely, and correct power and control adjustments to maintain proper pitch attitude and rate of descent to touchdown, touching down in the first one-third of the water landing area.
8. Contacts the water in the proper pitch attitude, and slows to idle taxi speed.
9. Maintains crosswind correction and directional control throughout the approach and landing sequence.

10. Completes the appropriate checklist.

Task G: *Rough Water Takeoff and Climb (AMES)*

NOTE: *If a rough water condition does not exist, the applicant shall be evaluated by simulating the Task.*

References: *FAA-H-8083-23, FAA-P-8740-19; POH/AFM.*

Objective: To determine that the applicant:

1. Exhibits satisfactory knowledge of the elements related to rough water takeoff and climb.
2. Positions the flight controls and flaps for the existing conditions.
3. Clears the area; selects an appropriate takeoff path considering wind, swells, surface hazards, and/or vessels.
4. Retracts the water rudders as appropriate; advances the throttle smoothly to takeoff power.
5. Establishes and maintains an appropriate planing attitude, directional control, and corrects for proposing, skipping, or excessive bouncing.
6. Lifts off at minimum airspeed and accelerates to V_Y, ±5 knots before leaving ground effect.
7. Retracts the landing gear, if appropriate, and flaps after a positive rate of climb is established.
8. Maintains takeoff power and V_Y ±5 knots to a safe maneuvering altitude.
9. Maintains directional control and proper wind-drift correction throughout takeoff and climb.
10. Completes the appropriate checklist.

Task H: *Rough Water Approach and Landing (AMES)*

NOTE: *If a rough water condition does not exist, the applicant shall be evaluated by simulating the Task.*

References: *FAA-H-8083-23; POH/AFM.*

Objective: To determine that the applicant:

1. Exhibits satisfactory knowledge of the elements related to rough water approach and landing.
2. Adequately surveys the intended landing area.
3. Considers the wind conditions, water, depth, hazards, surrounding terrain, and other watercraft.

4. Selects the most suitable approach path and touchdown area.
5. Establishes the recommended approach and landing configuration and airspeed, and adjusts pitch attitude and power as required.
6. Maintains a stabilized approach and the recommended approach airspeed, or in its absence not more than 1.3 V_{SO} ± 5 knots with wind gust factor applied.
7. Makes smooth, timely, and correct power and control application during the round out and touch down.
8. Contacts the water in the proper pitch attitude, and at the proper airspeed, considering the type of rough water.
9. Maintains crosswind correction and directional control throughout the approach and landing sequence.
10. Completes the appropriate checklist.

Task I: *Go-Around/Rejected Landing (AMEL and AMES)*

References: FAA-H-8083-3, FAA-H-8083-23; POH/AFM.

Objective: To determine that the applicant:

1. Exhibits satisfactory knowledge of the elements related to a go-around/rejected landing with emphasis on factors that contribute to landing conditions that may require a go-around.
2. Makes a timely decision to discontinue the approach to landing.
3. Applies takeoff power immediately and transitions to climb pitch attitude for V_X or V_Y as appropriate +10/–5 knots and/or appropriate pitch attitude.
4. Retracts flaps, as appropriate.
5. Retracts the landing gear if appropriate after a positive rate of climb is established.
6. Maneuvers to the side of runway/landing area to clear and avoid conflicting traffic.
7. Maintains takeoff power and V_Y ±5 knots to a safe maneuvering altitude.
8. Maintains directional control and proper wind-drift correction throughout the climb.
9. Completes the appropriate checklist.

V. Performance Maneuver

Task A: Steep Turns (AMEL and AMES)

References: FAA-H-8083-3; POH/AFM.

Objective: To determine that the applicant:

1. Exhibits satisfactory knowledge of the elements related to steep turns.
2. Establishes the manufacturer's recommended airspeed or if one is not stated, a safe airspeed not to exceed V_A.
3. Rolls into a coordinated 360° steep turn with at least a 50° bank, followed by a 360° steep turn in the opposite direction.
4. Divides attention between airplane control and orientation.
5. Maintains the entry altitude, ±100 feet, airspeed, ±10 knots, bank, ±5°; and rolls out on the entry heading, ±10°.

VI. Navigation

Task A: *Pilotage and Dead Reckoning (AMEL and AMES)*

References: FAA-H-8083-25; 14 CFR Part 61; Navigation Chart.

Objective: To determine that the applicant:

1. Exhibits satisfactory knowledge of the elements related to pilotage and dead reckoning.
2. Follows the preplanned course by reference to landmarks.
3. Identifies landmarks by relating surface features to chart symbols.
4. Navigates by means of precomputed headings, groundspeed, and elapsed time.
5. Demonstrates use of magnetic compass in navigation, to include turns to new headings.
6. Corrects for and records differences between preflight groundspeed, fuel consumption, and heading calculations and those determined en route.
7. Verifies the airplane's position within 2 nautical miles of flight planned route.
8. Arrives at the en route checkpoints within 3 minutes of the initial or revised ETA and provides a destination estimate.
9. Maintains appropriate altitude, ±100 feet and heading, ±10°.

Task B: *Navigation Systems and Radar Services (AMEL and AMES)*

References: FAA-H-8083-3, FAA-H-8083-6, FAA-H-8083-25; Navigation Equipment Operation Manuals; AIM.

Objective: To determine that the applicant:

1. Exhibits satisfactory knowledge of the elements related to navigation systems and radar services.
2. Demonstrates the ability to use an airborne electronic navigation system.
3. Locates the airplane's position using the navigation system.
4. Intercepts and tracks a given course, radial, or bearing as appropriate.
5. Recognizes and describes the indication of station passage, if appropriate.
6. Recognizes signal loss and takes appropriate action.
7. Uses proper communication procedures when utilizing radar services.

8. Maintains the appropriate altitude, ±100 feet and heading, ±10°.

Task C: Diversion (AMEL and AMES)

References: FAA-H-8083-25; AIM; Navigation Chart.

Objective: To determine that the applicant:

1. Exhibits satisfactory knowledge of the elements related to diversion.
2. Selects an appropriate alternate airport and route.
3. Makes an accurate estimate of heading, groundspeed, arrival time, and fuel consumption to the alternate airport.
4. Maintains the appropriate altitude, ±100 feet, and heading, ±10°.

Task D: Lost Procedures (AMEL and AMES)

References: FAA-H-8083-25; AIM; Navigation Chart.

Objective: To determine that the applicant:

1. Exhibits satisfactory knowledge of the elements related to lost procedures.
2. Selects an appropriate course of action.
3. Maintains an appropriate heading and climbs, if necessary.
4. Identifies prominent landmarks.
5. Uses navigation systems/facilities and/or contacts an ATC facility for assistance, as appropriate.

VII. Slow Flight and Stalls

NOTE: In accordance with FAA policy, all stalls for the Commercial Certificate/Rating will be taken to the "onset" (buffeting) stall condition.

Task A: *Maneuvering During Slow Flight (AMEL and AMES)*

References: FAA-H-8083-3; POH/AFM.

Objective: To determine that the applicant:

1. Exhibits satisfactory knowledge of the elements related to maneuvering during slow flight.
2. Selects an entry altitude that will allow the task to be completed no lower than 3,000 feet AGL.
3. Establishes and maintains an airspeed at which any further increase in angle of attack, increase in load factor, or reduction in power, would result in an immediate stall.
4. Accomplishes coordinated straight-and-level flight, turns, climbs, and descents with landing gear and flap configurations specified by the examiner.
5. Divides attention between airplane control and orientation.
6. Maintains the specified altitude, ±50 feet; specified heading, ±10°; airspeed +5/-0 knots, and specified angle of bank, ±5°.

Task B: *Power-Off Stalls (AMEL and AMES)*

References: FAA-H-8083-3; AC 61-67; POH/AFM.

Objective: To determine that the applicant:

1. Exhibits satisfactory knowledge of the elements related to power-off stalls.
2. Selects an entry altitude that allows the task to be completed no lower than 3,000 feet AGL.
3. Establishes a stabilized descent approximating a 3 degree final approach glidepath or landing decent rate in the approach or landing configuration, as specified by the examiner.
4. Transitions smoothly from the approach or landing attitude to a pitch attitude that will induce a stall.

5. Maintains a specified heading ±10°, in straight flight; maintains a specified angle of bank, not to exceed 20°, ±5°, in turning flight while inducing the stall.
6. Recognizes and recovers promptly at the "onset" (buffeting) stall condition.

NOTE: *Evaluation criteria for a recovery from an approach to stall should not mandate a predetermined value for altitude loss and should not mandate maintaining altitude during recovery. Proper evaluation criteria should consider the multitude of external and internal variables which affect the recovery altitude.*

7. Retracts the flaps to the recommended setting, retracts the landing gear, if retractable, after a positive rate of climb is established.
8. Accelerates to V_X or V_Y speed before the final flap retraction; returns to the maneuvering speed for the configuration or altitude, heading, and airspeed specified by the examiner.

Task C: Power-On Stalls (AMEL and AMES)

References: FAA-H-8083-3; AC 61-67; POH/AFM.

NOTE: *In some high performance airplanes as defined by 14 CFR part 61, the power setting may have to be reduced below the practical test standards guideline power setting to prevent excessively high pitch attitudes (greater than 30° nose up).*

Objective: To determine that the applicant:

1. Exhibits satisfactory knowledge of the elements related to power-on stalls.
2. Selects an entry altitude that allows the task to be completed no lower than 3,000 feet AGL.
3. Establishes the takeoff or departure configuration. Sets power to no less than 65 percent available power.
4. Transitions smoothly from the takeoff or departure attitude to a pitch attitude that will induce a stall.
5. Maintains a specified heading ±10°, in straight flight; maintains a specified angle of bank, not to exceed a 20°, ±10° in turning flight, while inducing the stall.
6. Recognizes and recovers promptly at the "onset" (buffeting) stall condition.

NOTE: *Evaluation criteria for a recovery from an approach to stall should not mandate a predetermined value for altitude loss and should not mandate maintaining altitude during recovery. Proper evaluation criteria should consider the multitude of external and internal variables which affect the recovery altitude.*

7. Retracts the flaps to the recommended setting, retracts the landing gear, if retractable, after a positive rate of climb is established.
8. Accelerates to V_X or V_Y speed before the final flap retraction; returns to the normal climb attitude, airspeed, and configuration or an altitude, heading, and airspeed specified by the examiner.

Task D: Accelerated Stalls (AMEL and AMES)

References: FAA-H-8083-3; AC 61-67; POH/AFM.

Objective: To determine that the applicant:

1. Exhibits satisfactory knowledge of the elements related to accelerated (power on or power off) stalls.
2. Selects an entry altitude that allows the task to be completed no lower than 3,000 feet AGL.
3. Establishes a steady flight condition and recommended airspeed established by the manufacturer, or in it's absence, not more than 1.2 V_S.
4. Transitions smoothly from the cruise attitude to the angle of bank of approximately 45° that will induce a stall.
5. Maintains coordinated turning flight, increasing elevator back pressure steadily and firmly to induce the stall.
6. Recognizes and recovers promptly at the "onset" (buffeting) stall condition.
7. Returns to the altitude, heading, and airspeed specified by the examiner.

Task E: Spin Awareness (AMEL and AMES)

References: FAA-H-8083-3; AC 61-67; POH/AFM.

Objective: To determine that the applicant exhibits knowledge of the elements related to spin awareness by explaining:

1. Aerodynamic factors related to spins.

2. Flight situations where unintentional spins may occur.
3. Procedures for recovery from unintentional spins.

VIII. Emergency Operations

NOTE: Examiners shall select an entry altitude that will allow the single engine demonstrations Task to be completed no lower than 3,000 feet AGL or the manufacturer's recommended altitude, whichever is higher. At altitudes lower than 3,000 feet AGL, engine failure shall be simulated by reducing throttle to idle and then establishing zero thrust.

Task A: Emergency Descent (AMEL and AMES)

References: FAA-H-8083-3; POH/AFM.

Objective: To determine that the applicant:

1. Exhibits satisfactory knowledge of the elements related to an emergency descent.
2. Recognizes situations, such as depressurization, cockpit smoke, and/or fire that require an emergency descent.
3. Establishes the appropriate airspeed and configuration for the emergency descent.
4. Exhibits orientation, division of attention, and proper planning.
5. Maintains positive load factors during the descent.
6. Completes appropriate checklists.
7. Maintains appropriate airspeed, +0/–10 knots and levels off at specified altitude, ±100 feet.

Task B: Engine Failure During Takeoff Before V_{MC} (Simulated) (AMEL and AMES)

References: FAA-H-8083-3, FAA-P-8740-19; POH/AFM.

NOTE: Engine failure (simulated) shall be accomplished before reaching 50 percent of the calculated V_{MC}.

Objective: To determine that the applicant:

1. Exhibits satisfactory knowledge of the elements related to the procedure used for engine failure during takeoff prior to reaching V_{MC}.
2. Closes the throttles smoothly and promptly when simulated engine failure occurs.
3. Maintains directional control and applies brakes (AMEL) or flight controls (AMES), as necessary.

Task C: *Engine Failure After Lift-Off (Simulated) (AMEL and AMES)*

NOTE: *Simulated engine failure of the most critical engine shall be demonstrated after liftoff. However, the failure of an engine shall not be simulated until attaining at least VSSE/VXSE/VYSE and at an altitude not lower than 500 feet AGL.*

References: FAA-H-8083-3, FAA-P-8740-19; POH/AFM.

Objective: To determine that the applicant:

1. Exhibits satisfactory knowledge of the elements related to the procedure used for engine failure after lift-off.
2. Recognizes a simulated engine failure promptly, maintains control, and utilizes appropriate manufacturer's emergency procedures.
3. Reduces drag, identifies and verifies the inoperative engine after simulated engine failure.
4. Simulates feathering the propeller on the inoperative engine. Examiner shall then establish zero-thrust on the inoperative engine.
5. Establishes V_{YSE}; if obstructions are present, establishes V_{XSE} or V_{MC} +5 knots, whichever is greater, until obstructions are cleared. Then transitions to V_{YSE}.
6. Banks toward the operating engine as required for best performance.
7. Monitors operating engine and makes adjustments, as necessary.
8. Recognizes the airplane's performance capabilities. If a climb is not possible at V_{YSE}, maintain V_{YSE} and return to the departure airport for landing, or initiates an approach to the most suitable landing area available.
9. Simulates securing the inoperative engine.
10. Maintains heading, ±10°, and airspeed, ±5 knots.
11. Completes appropriate emergency checklist.

Task D: *Approach and Landing with an Inoperative Engine (Simulated) (AMEL and AMES)*

References: FAA-H-8083-3, FAA-P-8740-19; POH/AFM.

Objective: To determine that the applicant:

1. Exhibits satisfactory knowledge of the elements related to an approach and landing with an engine inoperative to include engine failure on final approach.
2. Recognizes engine failure and takes appropriate action, maintains control, and utilizes manufacturer's recommended emergency procedures.
3. Banks toward the operating engine, as required, for best performance.
4. Monitors the operating engine and makes adjustments as necessary.
5. Maintains the manufacturer's recommended approach airspeed ±5 knots, and landing configuration with a stabilized approach, until landing is assured.
6. Makes smooth, timely, and correct control applications during round out and touchdown.
7. Touches down on the first one-third of available runway, with no drift and the airplane's longitudinal axis aligned with and over the runway center/landing path.
8. Maintains crosswind correction and directional control throughout the approach and landing sequence.
9. Completes appropriate checklists.

Task E: Systems and Equipment Malfunctions (AMEL and AMES)

References: FAA-H-8083-3; POH/AFM.

Objective: To determine that the applicant:

1. Exhibits knowledge of the elements related to systems and equipment malfunctions appropriate to the airplane provided for the practical test.
2. Analyzes the situation and takes appropriate action for simulated emergencies appropriate to the airplane provided for the practical test for at least three of the following—

   a. partial or complete power loss.
   b. engine roughness or overheat.
   c. carburetor or induction icing.
   d. loss of oil pressure.
   e. fuel starvation.
   f. electrical malfunction.
   g. vacuum/pressure, and associated flight instruments malfunction.
   h. pitot/static system malfunction.
   i. landing gear or flap malfunction.

j. inoperative trim.
k. inadvertent door or window opening.
l. structural icing.
m. smoke/fire/engine compartment fire.
n. any other emergency appropriate to the airplane.

3. Follows the appropriate checklist or procedure.

Task F: *Emergency Equipment and Survival Gear (AMEL and AMES)*

References: FAA-H-8083-3; POH/AFM.

Objective: To determine that the applicant:

1. Exhibits knowledge of the elements related to emergency equipment and survival gear appropriate to the airplane and environment encountered during flight. Identifies appropriate equipment that should be onboard the airplane.

IX. High Altitude Operations

Task A: Supplemental Oxygen (AMEL and AMES)

References: 14 CFR part 91; FAA-H-8083-3, FAA-H-8083-25; AC 61-107; AIM; POH/AFM.

Objective: To determine that the applicant exhibits knowledge of the elements related to supplemental oxygen by explaining:

1. Supplemental oxygen requirements for flight crew and passengers when operating non-pressurized airplanes.
2. Identification and differences between "aviator's breathing oxygen" and other types of oxygen.
3. Operational characteristics of continuous flow, demand, and pressure-demand oxygen systems.

Task B: Pressurization (AMEL and AMES)

References: FAA-H-8083-3, FAA-H-8083-25; AC 61-107; AIM; POH/AFM.

Objective: To determine that the applicant:

1. Exhibits knowledge of the elements related to pressurization by explaining—

   a. fundamental concept of cabin pressurization.
   b. supplemental oxygen requirements when operating airplanes with pressurized cabins.
   c. physiological hazards associated with high altitude flight and decompression.

NOTE: Element 2 applies only if the airplane provided for the practical test is equipped for pressurized flight operations.

2. Operates the pressurization system properly, and reacts appropriately to simulated pressurization malfunctions.

X. Multiengine Operations

NOTE: *If the applicant does not hold an instrument rating airplane, Tasks C and D need not to be accomplished. All other tasks need to be completed.*

Task A: Maneuvering with One Engine Inoperative (AMEL and AMES)

References: FAA-H-8083-3, FAA-P-8740-19; POH/AFM.

NOTE: *The feathering of one propeller shall be demonstrated in flight, unless the manufacturer prohibits the intentional feathering of the propellers during flight. The maneuver shall be performed at altitudes above 3,000 feet AGL or the manufacturer's recommended altitude, whichever is higher, and positions where safe landings on established airports can be readily accomplished. In the event a propeller cannot be unfeathered during the practical test, it shall be treated as an emergency.*

Objective: To determine that the applicant:

1. Exhibits satisfactory knowledge of the elements related to maneuvering with one engine inoperative.
2. Recognizes engine failure and maintains control.
3. Sets the engine controls, reduces drag, identifies and verifies the inoperative engine, and feathers appropriate propeller.
4. Establishes and maintains a bank toward the operating engine as required for best performance in straight-and-level flight.
5. Follows the manufacturer's prescribed checklists to verify procedures for securing the inoperative engine.
6. Monitors the operating engine and makes necessary adjustments.
7. Demonstrates coordinated flight with one engine inoperative (propeller feathered).
8. Restarts the inoperative engine using manufacturer's appropriate restart procedures.
9. Maintains altitude ±100 feet or minimum sink, as appropriate, and heading ±10°.
10. Completes the appropriate checklists.

Task B: V_{MC} Demonstration (AMEL and AMES)

References: FAA-H-8083-3, FAA-P-8740-19; POH/AFM.

NOTE: An applicant seeking an airplane—multiengine land (AMEL) rating, "Limited to Center Thrust," is not required to be evaluated on this Task.

NOTE: Airplanes with normally aspirated engines will lose power as altitude increases because of the reduced density of the air entering the induction system of the engine. This loss of power will result in a V_{MC} lower than the stall speed at higher altitudes. Therefore, recovery should be made at the first indication of loss of directional control, stall warning, or buffet. Do not perform this maneuver by increasing the pitch attitude to a high angle with both engines operating and then reducing power on the critical engine. This technique is hazardous and may result in loss of airplane control.

Objective: To determine that the applicant:

1. Exhibits satisfactory knowledge of the elements related to V_{MC} by explaining the causes of loss of directional control at airspeeds less than V_{MC}, the factors affecting V_{MC}, and safe recovery procedures.

2. Configures the airplane in accordance with the manufacturer's recommendation, in the absence of the manufacturer's recommendations, then at V_{SSE}/V_{YSE}, as appropriate—

   a. Landing gear retracted.
   b. Flaps set for takeoff.
   c. Cowl flaps set for takeoff.
   d. Trim set for takeoff.
   e. Propellers set for high RPM.
   f. Power on critical engine reduced to idle.
   g. Power on operating engine set to takeoff or maximum available power.

3. Establishes a single-engine climb attitude with the airspeed at approximately 10 knots above V_{SSE} or V_{YSE}, as appropriate.

4. Establishes a bank toward the operating engine, as required for best performance and controllability.

5. Increases the pitch attitude slowly to reduce the airspeed at approximately 1 knot per second while applying rudder pressure to maintain directional control until full rudder is applied.

6. Recognizes indications of loss of directional control, stall warning, or buffet.
7. Recovers promptly by simultaneously reducing power sufficiently on the operating engine while decreasing the angle of attack as necessary to regain airspeed and directional control. Recovery SHOULD NOT be attempted by increasing the power on the simulated failed engine.
8. Recovers within 20° of the entry heading.
9. Advances power smoothly on operating engine and accelerates to V_{XSE}/V_{YSE}, as appropriate, ±5 knots, during the recovery.

Task C: Engine Failure During Flight (By Reference to Instruments) (AMEL and AMES)

References: 14 CFR part 61; FAA-H-8083-3, FAA-H-8083-15.

Objective: To determine that the applicant:

1. Exhibits satisfactory knowledge of the elements by explaining the procedures used during instrument flight with one engine inoperative.
2. Recognizes engine failure, sets the engine controls, reduces drag, identifies, and verifies the inoperative engine, and simulates feathering appropriate engine propeller.
3. Establishes and maintains a bank toward the operating engine as required for best performance in straight-and-level.
4. Follows the prescribed manufacturer's checklists to verify procedures for securing the inoperative engine.
5. Monitors the operating engine and makes necessary adjustments.
6. Demonstrates coordinated flight with one engine inoperative.
7. Maintains altitude ±100 feet or minimum sink, as appropriate, and heading ±10°, bank ±5°, and levels off from climbs and descents within ±100 feet.

Task D: Instrument Approach—One Engine Inoperative (By Reference to Instruments) (AMEL and AMES)

References: 14 CFR part 61; FAA-H-8083-3, FAA S-8081-4; AC 61-27.

Objective: To determine that the applicant:

1. Exhibits satisfactory knowledge of the elements by explaining the procedures used during a published instrument approach with one engine inoperative.
2. Recognizes engine failure, sets the engine controls, reduces drag, identifies and verifies the simulated inoperative engine, and simulates feathering the appropriate engine propeller.
3. Establishes and maintains a bank toward the operating engine, as required, for best performance in straight-and-level.
4. Follows the manufacturer's prescribed checklists to verify procedures for securing the inoperative engine.
5. Monitors the operating engine and makes necessary adjustments.
6. Requests and receives an actual or a simulated ATC clearance for an instrument approach.
7. Follows the actual or a simulated ATC clearance for an instrument approach.
8. Maintains altitude within 100 feet, the airspeed within ±10 knots if within the aircraft's capability, and heading ±10°.
9. Establishes a rate of descent that will ensure arrival at the MDA or DH/DA, with the airplane in a position from which a descent to a landing, on the intended runway can be made, either straight in or circling as appropriate.
10. On final approach segment, no more than three-quarter-scale deflection of the CDI/glide slope indicator. For RMI or ADF indicators, within 10° of the course.
11. Avoids loss of aircraft control, or attempted flight contrary to the engine-inoperative operating limitations of the aircraft.
12. Complies with the published criteria for the aircraft approach category when circling.
13. Completes landing and manufacturer's appropriate checklists.

XI. Postflight Procedures

Task A: *After Landing, Parking, and Securing (AMEL and AMES)*

NOTE: *The examiner shall select Task A and for AMES applicants at least one other Task.*

References: FAA-H-8083-3, FAA-H-8083-23; POH/AFM.

Objective: To determine that the applicant:

1. Exhibits satisfactory knowledge of the elements related to after landing, parking, and securing procedures.
2. Maintains directional control after touchdown while decelerating to an appropriate speed.
3. Observes runway hold lines and other surface control markings and lighting.
4. Parks in an appropriate area, considering the safety of nearby persons and property.
5. Follows the appropriate procedure for engine shutdown.
6. Completes the appropriate checklist.
7. Conducts an appropriate post flight inspection and secures the aircraft.

Task B: *Anchoring (AMES)*

References: FAA-H-8083-23; POH/AFM.

Objective: To determine that the applicant:

1. Exhibits satisfactory knowledge of the elements related to anchoring.
2. Selects a suitable area for anchoring, considering seaplane movement, water depth, tide, wind, and weather changes.
3. Uses an adequate number of anchors and lines of sufficient strength and length to ensure the seaplane's security.

Task C: *Docking and Mooring (AMES)*

References: FAA-H-8083-23; POH/AFM.

Objective: To determine that the applicant:

1. Exhibits satisfactory knowledge of the elements related to docking and mooring.

2. Approaches the dock or mooring buoy in the proper direction considering speed, hazards, wind, and water current.
3. Ensures seaplane security.

Task D: Ramping/Beaching (AMES)

References: FAA-H-8083-23; POH/AFM.

Objective: To determine that the applicant:

1. Exhibits satisfactory knowledge of the elements related to ramping/beaching.
2. Approaches the ramp/beach considering persons and property, in the proper attitude and direction, at a safe speed, considering water depth, tide, current, and wind.
3. Ramps/beaches and secures the seaplane in a manner that will protect it from the harmful effect of wind, waves, and changes in water level.

Appendix 2

Task vs. Simulation Device Credit

Multiengine Land (MEL)

Airplane Multiengine Land

Task vs. Simulation Device Credit

Examiners conducting the Commercial Pilot–Airplane Practical Tests with flight simulation devices should consult appropriate documentation to ensure that the device has been approved for training, testing, or checking. The documentation for each device should reflect that the following activities have occurred:

1. The device must be evaluated, determined to meet the appropriate standards, and assigned the appropriate qualification level by the National Simulator Program Manager. The device must continue to meet qualification standards through continuing evaluations as outlined in the appropriate advisory circular (AC) or 14 CFR part 60. For airplane flight training devices (FTDs), AC 120-45 (as amended), Airplane Flight Training Device Qualifications, will be used. For simulators, AC 120-40 (as amended), Airplane Simulator Qualification, or part 60 will be used.

2. The FAA must approve the device for training, testing, and checking the specific flight Tasks listed in this appendix.

3. The device must continue to support the level of student or applicant performance required by the PTS.

NOTE: *Users of the following chart are cautioned that use of the chart alone is incomplete. The description and objective of each Task as listed in the body of the PTS, including all notes, must also be incorporated for accurate simulation device use.*

Use of Chart

X   Creditable.
A   Creditable if appropriate systems are installed and operating.
*   Asterisk items require use of FTD or Simulator visual reference.

NOTES:

1. Use of Level 1, 2 or Level 3 FTDs is not authorized for the practical test required by this PTS.

2. For practical tests, not more than 50 % of the maneuvers may be accomplished in an FTD or simulator UNLESS:

   a. each maneuver has been satisfactorily accomplished for an instructor, in the appropriate airplane, not less than three (3) times,

OR

   b. the applicant has logged not less than 500 hours of flight time as a pilot in airplanes.

3. Not all Areas of Operation (AOO) and Tasks required by this PTS are listed in the appendix. The remaining AOO and Tasks must be accomplished in an airplane.

Multiengine Land

125

FAA-S-8081-12C

(this page intentionally left blank)

Flight Simulation Device Level

Areas of Operation	Flight Simulation Device Level							
	4	5	6	7	A	B	C	D
II. Preflight Procedures								
A. Preflight Inspection (Cockpit Only)	A	A	X	X	X	X	X	X
B. Cockpit Management	A	A	X	X	X	X	X	X
C. Engine Starting	A	A	X	X	X	X	X	X
D. Taxiing								
G. Before Takeoff Check	A	A	X	X	X	X	X	X
IV. Takeoffs, Landings, and Go-Arounds								
A. Normal and Crosswind Takeoff and Climb	—	—	—	—	—	—	X	X
B. Normal and Crosswind Approach and Landing	—	—	—	—	—	—	X	X
E. Short-Field Takeoff and Climb	—	—	—	—	X	X	X	X
F. Short-Field Approach and Landing	—	—	—	—	—	—	X	X
L. Go-Around*/Rejected Landing	—	—	X	X	X	X	X	X
V. Performance Maneuvers								
A. Steep Turns	—	—	X	X	X	X	X	X
VI. Navigation*								
B. Navigation Systems and Radar Services	—	A	X	X	X	X	X	X
C. Diversion	—	A	X	X	X	X	X	X
D. Lost Procedures	—	A	X	X	X	X	X	X

127

Multiengine Land

(this page intentionally left blank)

Flight Simulation Device Level

Areas of Operation	Flight Simulation Device Level							
	4	5	6	7	A	B	C	D
VII. Slow Flight and Stalls								
A. Maneuvering During Slow Flight	–	–	X	X	X	X	X	X
VIII. Emergency Operations								
A. Emergency Descent	–	–	X	X	X	X	X	X
B. Engine Failure During Takeoff Before V_{MC}	–	–	–	–	X	X	X	X
C. Engine Failure After Lift-Off (Simulated)	–	–	–	–	X	X	X	X
D. Approach and Landing with Inoperative Engine (Simulated)	A	A	X	X	X	X	X	X
E. Systems and Equipment Malfunctions	A	A	X	X	X	X	X	X
IX. High Altitude Operations								
B. Pressurization	A	A	X	X	X	X	X	X
X. Multiengine Operations								
C. Engine Failure During Flight (By reference to instruments)	–	–	X	X	X	X	X	X
D. Instrument Approach – One Engine Inoperative (By reference to instruments)	–	–	–	–	X	X	X	X
XI. Postflight Procedures								
A. After Landing, Parking, and Securing	A	A	X	X	X	X	X	X

129

Multiengine Land